Waterwise Gardening

Waterwise Gardening

EVERYTHING YOU NEED TO KNOW ABOUT EFFICIENT WATERING TO GROW A HEALTHY YARD

Richard Restuccia

First published in the United States of America in 2025
by Rizzoli International Publications, Inc.
49 West 27th Street
New York, NY 10001
www.rizzoliusa.com

Publisher: Charles Miers
Editor: Stacee Gravelle Lawrence
Design: Kelley Galbreath
Production Manager: Rebecca Ambrose
Managing Editor: Lynn Scrabis

ISBN: 978-0-8478-4689-4
Library of Congress Control Number: 2024946656

Printed in China
2025 2026 2027 2028 / 10 9 8 7 6 5 4 3 2 1

Visit us online:
Instagram.com/RizzoliBooks
Facebook.com/RizzoliNewYork
X: @Rizzoli_Books
Youtube.com/user/RizzoliNY

Contents

1

Act
Now

PEOPLE ARE SOMETIMES SURPRISED WHEN they learn we have clean water scarcity issues in the United States; we most certainly do. There are seven common causes of water scarcity: drought, population growth, climate change, water pollution, inefficient water use, aging infrastructure, and over extraction of groundwater. Commercial agriculture is using most of the water, though residential landscape water use gets most of the media attention. Quickly escalating water rates that have been outpacing inflation in other areas also impact home gardeners and homeowners the most.

A recent example of water scarcity that rightfully became national news because of its impact on everyday citizens is what took place in Flint, Michigan. The municipality experienced known water issues for over six years. In 2014, the town's water supply was shifted from sources in Lake Huron and the Detroit River over to the Flint River in a cost-saving move. The Flint River water had long been contaminated by waste from industries such as car factories, meatpacking plants, paper mills, agriculture, and landfills. It was inadequately tested or treated before being piped into homes, which caused severe problems for residents. High levels of lead leached into the drinking water supply, and around 100,000 people were exposed to elevated lead levels, with children bearing the brunt of the impact. Residents had to find other ways to cook, clean, and bathe because they did not have clean running water for years, and it wasn't until citizens organized to draw attention to the problem that officials acknowledged it and were forced to take action. Ultimately, Congress had to step in with a major grant to help the city bring the water and its piping system back into compliance with Department of Health guidelines.

Similarly, the town of St. Joseph, Louisiana, has experienced water problems including elevated levels of lead and copper for years due to a poorly maintained and deteriorating water distribution system. The governor declared it a public health emergency in 2016 it is still recommended that residents today use an alternative water source to tap water for personal consumption, ice making, toothbrushing, and food preparation. The population of this town has been shrinking for the last thirty years, and the current population of just over 1,100 people makes maintaining a high-quality system expensive for the city.

Scarcity caused by drought currently affects several small towns in the Central Valley of California (even after significant rainfall in 2023), which are experiencing dry wells and no running water. In Arizona, the unincorporated town of Rio Verde Foothills in Maricopa County has been experiencing drought so severe that though many residents have private wells, about five hundred residents still have had to rely on water hauled from Scottsdale. Scottsdale cut the water supply off in early 2023, and now residents will be on their own for water for at least a couple of years. Many have to drive an hour away to pay to get tanks filled at almost four times the price they were paying before. The mayor of Scottsdale, David Ortega, said, "Water is not a compassion game." I couldn't disagree more.

We will all have to make some sacrifices to solve water scarcity issues. The first step is understanding the seven common causes of water scarcity to learn how we can work together to reduce the impact of the issues.

1 **Drought**—Periods of prolonged dry weather reduce water availability to specific regions. Today, with increasingly unpredictable weather, an area that normally receives plenty of water can switch to being in a drought crisis with just a couple of years of drier weather. This is becoming more common and more challenging to manage.

2 **Population Growth**—People are increasingly moving to the Southwest states in the U.S., though most don't consider the availability or cost of water there. The big challenge with water and explosive population growth is that the same city governments who are responsible for honest assessments and management of water supply are also responsible for attracting new residents that bring economic prosperity. There is a built-in conflict of interest.

3 **Climate Change**—This goes hand in hand with drought. Changing rain patterns make supply unpredictable. This past winter in California, for example, was an instance of too much rain falling in too short of a period, which led to severe flooding. Currently, there is no way to capture such an excess of water and convincing taxpayers to fund water storage construction projects to accommodate rogue water years is a difficult proposition.

4 **Water Pollution**—Industrial waste or agricultural runoff can impact residential areas and supply quickly. Contaminants are a serious issue, and are caused by both by large companies and individuals to different degrees.

5 **Inefficient Water Use**—Inefficient irrigation systems for agriculture and urban areas are significant contributors to water scarcity issues. In the West, agriculture uses around 80% of the available water. Implementing smart irrigation systems and harnessing technology that is readily available at a reasonable price will go a long way to help solve water scarcity issues.

6 **Aging Infrastructure**—A 2020 Stanford University study estimates that 20% to 50% of water is simply lost due to leaks in North America's supply system.

7 **Over-extraction of Groundwater**—Pumping out groundwater faster than water tables can be replenished naturally is a big issue. Agricultural growing practices that use drip irrigation, for example, slow the over pumping of groundwater by reducing the amount of water needed and/or wasted.

This is not a complete list of issues pertaining to contemporary water usage, of course. The challenges tend to vary from region to region, but raising awareness of the issues, learning from past challenges, and encouraging everyone to make individual efforts to reduce water usage is key to ensuring these problems don't adversely affect your community.

Insist the People Who Use the Most Water Save the Most Water

According to the World Bank, agriculture accounts for 70% of all freshwater withdrawals globally. In California, around 80% of the water is used for agriculture. This means that a large portion of the water in California is used to grow crops and support farming. Similarly, about 78% of the water in Nevada is used for agriculture. In Arizona, approximately 74% of the water is used for agriculture. In Texas, around 57% of the water is used for agriculture. Lastly, an estimated 97% of the water is used for agriculture in Idaho. These statistics highlight the significant reliance on water for agricultural activities in these states, and while agriculture is important for food production and state economies, it's still important to emphasize the importance of water management and conservation strategies to ensure the sustainable use of this valuable resource.

The Environmental Protection Agency estimates approximately 8 billion gallons are used daily in the United States for residential landscape irrigation. On its own, that is a number that is hard to comprehend. Considering that 322 billion gallons of water are used daily in the U.S. overall, the 8 billion gallons used for landscape irrigation only total 2.5% of our water use, but this area receives disproportionate attention.

Across the United States, most of the visible push to conserve water is focused on urban areas, specifically landscape water use, and while raising consciousness over any and all water use is worthwhile, incentives that may be popular with voters don't always translate into real-world results. Several states across the country offer rebates to remove turf grass, for example. A couple of states have even taken steps to create laws to eliminate turf grass in nonfunctional areas completely.

Turf grass is expensive to remove. The rebates offered by government agencies are excessive, proportionately speaking. Homeowners can receive over $125,000 an acre in some states for turf removal, only for the grass to be replaced with another plant that also requires watering. The ultimate water savings are insignificant, and the incentive and costs are high. The plants replacing the

turf are often watered with an inefficient irrigation system, and the water waste cycle continues—it's only people's perception that the issues are being addressed in effective ways. To cite a parallel social issue, when car accidents became one of the leading causes of death in the United States, the solution was not to ban cars. The solution was to use technology to improve safety standards, and this was very successful in reducing deaths. Many less expensive and less restrictive ways to reduce landscape water use exist aside from removing turf grass.

Making changes in how we water instead of what we water and providing incentives for managing water will get the reductions we need to conserve water in appreciable ways. In addition, we would free up some of the rebate money earmarked for reducing turf for better use for incentives to reduce water used for the agriculture industry, where it can make a more significant difference to our national and global supply. Imagine offering farmers the same type of incentives. A simple drip irrigation system can be installed for a few thousand dollars per acre. The rebate dollars currently allotted for turf removal would go much further for agricultural incentives and help the people using the most water save the most water.

In pursuing efficient water management straetgies and policies, it is crucial to critically evaluate our focus areas for maximizing water conservation efforts. While landscape irrigation has often been singled out as a prime targct for reduction, such a singular focus will yield little water savings in the broader context. Instead, we must expand our perspectives and explore alternative solutions to significantly impact water conservation.

Skyrocketing Water Rates May Aid Conservation Efforts

The High Cost of Water

I admit that, back in the day, I may have thought of my own father as being cheap for not wanting to water the lawn. If he were alive today, however, I would not call him cheap—I would call him green, sustainable, or maybe a conservationist. I was reminded of this as I spoke to an old friend recently who told me, "I don't waste anything because I don't want to waste money." Twenty years ago, we would also have called him cheap, or frugal on a good day. Fortunately, our outlook has changed, and whatever the reason for not wasting resources (whether altruistic or selfish), we celebrate anyone who acts in a green way. Soaring water rate hikes nationwide will necessarily drive some home gardeners to conserve water, simply because people want to save money. The growing awareness of our impact on the environment is an additional bonus.

10 Facts About Water

1   The Earth contains the same amount of water today as when the planet was first formed.

2   Today's tap water could contain the same molecules that our ancient ancestors also used or drank thousands of years ago. (Ewww factor or cool factor?)

3   Frozen water is lighter than water by about 9%, which is why ice floats.

4   If the world population continues to grow at the current rate, by the end of the century the world will have over 10 billion people. (There are over 7 billion people today.) Feeding this many people will require more food to be grown in the next 75 years than all the food ever produced in human history. This food will need lots of water—and therefore more efficient methods of irrigation to make such production levels achievable.

5   Most Americans find this hard to believe, but a quarter of the world's population does not have access to safe drinking water.

6   Are you singing in the shower? Next time you shower, think about this instead: Two-thirds of the water used in a home is used in the bathroom. Older toilets can use up to seven gallons of water per flush. At five flushes per day, that is almost 13,000 gallons per year. Federal plumbing standards specify new toilets can only use 1.6 gallons per flush, for 3,000 gallons per year. That is still a lot of clean drinking water per flush and begs the question of why we use clean drinking water (instead of gray water) in our toilets at all.

7   In a five-minute shower, we use 25 to 50 gallons of water. If you take a Navy shower, you keep this to around 3 gallons of water. That is a boatload of savings.

8   It is called hard water when water contains a lot of calcium and magnesium. Hard water accelerates the demise of cooling towers and boilers. In homes, we like to soften hard water, but in turn that causes issues for our plants.

9   A person can live about three weeks without food but only about three days without water.

10 The United States uses nearly 80% of its water for irrigation and thermoelectric power.

According to a Grant Thornton report in 2014, saving money is the number-one reason executives provide for moving companies to more environmentally sustainable business practices. We are experiencing this in our home gardens as well. As water rates increase, gardeners ask how they can save water and money. However, the way most water bills are structured complicates the average home-owner's understanding of how much they actually pay for water and how much they actually use—all we recognize when we get the bill is that it seems to be a lot. Across the 50 largest metropolitan areas in the U.S., monthly household water bills average $45.44, and monthly wastewater bills average $66.20, based on average household consumption across the country. Combined household water and wastewater bills have increased an average of 4.2% per year over the past nine years. This is a 46% increase in your water bill over the last nine years.

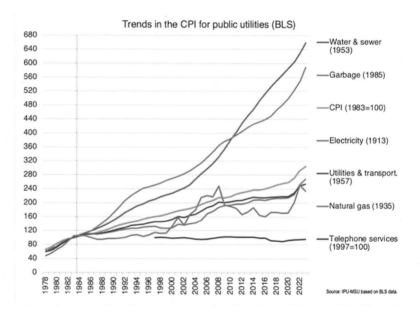

The water billing process in the U.S. is confusing. Most bills are calculated on two-month periods, and it takes a few weeks beyond the end of the billing cycle for utilities to generate invoices. As a result, the water bill you receive reporting water use sometimes reflects usage from 80 or 90 days prior. It's hard to see if you need to make a change with the delay between when you use the water and when you understand how much you used and the cost. Water bills could be more straight-forward and less complicated for consumers to understand, but due to necessary and more intricate water price structures, they get more complicated daily. Ask someone what the current price of a gallon of gas is for their car, and they can likely respond in a few seconds. Ask the same person how much they are paying for a gallon of water and you'll receive a blank stare. Give them their water bill and a calculator, and they may be able to discern the average price in 10 to 15 minutes, or not at all. Ask them how much water they use per month, and you will receive a similar shrug. It's not just the delay in bills that creates the problem. It is the bill itself. To be able to conserve water, it is essential to know how much you use and how much you pay for water. We all know the quote, "If you can't measure it, you can't manage it." In the case of water, we are doing a great job of measuring it, but interpreting the data about cost per gallon can be difficult.

Traditional Water Rate Calculations

One traditional way of pricing water is a monthly flat, or fixed-rate, charge for water. For example, many homes in Sacramento, California, pay a fixed rate for water. It doesn't matter how much or how little water they use, the municipality has decided a way to average out the cost over all consumers, so each household is charged the same amount every month. Most fixed-rate water structures charge a nominal amount for water, and the homes in these jurisdictions won't even have a meter, so the opportunity for waste is very high. Another traditional pricing is the simple uniform rate. Consumers pay the same amount for each gallon of water they use. It sounds simple, but where this gets tricky is determining how much water you use. Almost all water bills quote the amount of water in HCF or CCF, not gallons.

- **HCF** stands for 100 cubic feet of water. There are 748 gallons of water in 100 cubic feet. When your bill reads 6 HCF, multiply six by 748 to get 4,488 gallons of water.

- **CCF** also stands for 100 cubic feet of water. The first C is the Roman numeral "C" for 100. The following CF is cubic feet. Once again, you must multiply the units by 748 to know how much you pay a gallon.

Typically, water agencies also charge a water base fee or meter charge in addition to your water use charge. Almost all also add a sewer charge. A sewer charge should not apply to water used for landscapes, though, and if you have a separate meter for your landscape water, you should not be paying a sewer fee for that water. This is very important because a sewer charge can often be equal to the price of water. Therefore, installing a separate meter for your irrigation lines could measure what water goes where and save you thousands of dollars a year. Be sure to talk with your water agency before you add a meter for your landscape water to ensure they can acknowledge or measure your usage appropriately.

The Simple Tiered Water Bill

In a tiered pricing structure, consumers pay more as they use more. The tiered pricing increases in steps as more water is used. Below is a typical tiered water price structure:

TIER	AMOUNT IN GALLONS	PRICE PER 1,000 GALLONS
Tier 1	0—8,000	$4.79
Tier 2	8,001—22,000	$5.51
Tier 3	22,001—30,000	$6.88
Tier 4	Over 30,000	$10.33

Notice that the tiered rates are per 1,000 gallons, not CCF or HCF. The fixed fees discussed above also apply to tiered-rate pricing. Your tiered-rate pricing will vary depending on whether the property is single-family, commercial, or multi-family housing.

Budgeted Tiered-Water Bill

A water-budgeted tiered rate structure is sometimes called a "goal system allocated system" or "customer-specific water rate." For water budget tiered rates, the water utility determines how much water a given consumer will likely use, based on variables such as the landscape's square footage, daily weather and climate, and season of the year, as well as the number of people in the household. A water budget or goal is established, and then, depending on whether the resident uses more or less than estimated budget for the property, the final bill is calculated. Below is an example of a tiered water budget rate schedule:

TIER	AMOUNT OF BUDGET	PRICE PER 1000 GALLONS
Tier 1: Excellent Use	75%	$2.49
Tier 2: Efficient Use	76%–100%	$4.29
Tier 3: Inefficient	101%–140%	$8.79
Tier 4: Excessive	Over 140%	$16.41

In this example, it is easy to see how conservation is rewarded by significantly lower water rates in Tiers 1 and 2.

Water agencies around the country have devised many variations of this rate schedule. I have seen consumers placed into the excessive categories at a much lower percentage of the budget, for example, depending on the region, making the incentive for conservation high. As water agencies have begun adopting this structure, they have been very generous with the budgets they have implemented. In the future, we will see stricter budgets and higher percentage increases as water use surpasses the utility's overall water budget.

As a homeowner, building owner, or manager, it is essential to know what type of water rate structure your property is under. It is also necessary to carefully manage the system. Monthly or weekly meter readings and smart controllers, with flow sensing, can help you determine consumption in real time and help you make adjustments to stay in the lower tiers. Water bills have been complicated in the past and are getting more complex, but a thorough understanding and monitoring of the bills will pay off.

Learning from Past Water Issues

Water crisis officials in Cape Town, South Africa, saw the signs of an impending water crisis but chose to hope past weather patterns would return rain to the area and the crises would be resolved instead of planning for the worst-case scenario. But between 2015 and 2018, the city of 4 million people was restricted to using 13 gallons of water per person per day (compare this to the U.S., where the average is over 100 gallons per person per day), making it the first likely major city in the world to get to the brink of running dry. Cape Town is a thriving major modern city, responsible for 9.9% of South Africa's GDP. Cape Town is the size of San Diego, California—imagine San Diego going dry. In 2014 Cape Town's water supplies were at full capacity, but just three years of drought brought it to the brink of emergency.

I hear similar rhetoric in the dry Western United States today, where we hope a drought will end without any evidence that it will. Improved water supply, sanitation, and water resources management boost cities' and the country's economic growth, so who wants to be responsible for ringing the alarm bell saying any given town will have a water crisis sometime in the near future? There's little upside to it, and it could rain. There is more upside in promoting a city's sustainability plan to benefit businesses wanting to relocate.

For example, Phoenix, Arizona's population has grown 23% in the past ten years. Phoenix added more than 32,000 people between July 2015 and July 2016. That was the most for any city in the United States. During the same period, Los

Angeles added more than 27,000 and New York 21,000. Phoenix is proud of its water infrastructure. For a while, the City of Phoenix advertised on their website that the State of Arizona assured the city a water supply for the next hundred years. People won't readily move to places with known water issues, so this was an important piece of advertising for the community. Most cities face the challenges of attracting more residents and assuring them the basics like power and water are plentiful is key. It's hard for cities to see this in an unbiased way. Today, however, this information has been removed from the City of Phoenix website, but I wonder how many were satisfied by the hundred-year water supply guarantee and moved to Phoenix thinking they would be okay. The drought has now gone on for 23 years and is the worst in 110 years of recordkeeping. It's become dependent on Colorado River water levels instead of solely groundwater levels; both are declining.

What Can Individuals Do about the Water Crisis?

Demand Unbiased Water Supply Estimates

Most assume the cities they live in or move to will always have plentiful water supplies. Water awareness is improving, but we need better water supply estimates for large urban areas in the U.S. With technology today, receiving a report for the expected water supply in the future is not unreasonable. This may be a business opportunity . . . !

Have Foresight

Learn about what constitutes and then supports prudent legislation. We need legislation to help states catch and retain more water. We also need to support funding for desalinization plants and recycled water. We need to adjust our eating habits and learn how to use water more efficiently. It's going to take many small solutions to create one large solution.

You can do the same on your property. Make whatever changes you are able to implement today. Water-saving devices like smart controllers and rain sensors should be standard on every property. Install some to help your municipality avoid the kinds of big problems other cities have had to deal with recently.

Practice Performance-Based vs. Prescription-Based Water Management

Advocate for your water utility to make people responsible for water use reduction. Ask them to provide a target to hit, then insist people work to hit that target. Residents can decide whether to use drip irrigation, smart controllers, or pull out their lawn, so long as they take some demonstrated step to reduce usage—a little of all three or one of the many other ways to save water in your landscape discussed elsewhere in this book. That's not too tall an order. Today, new climate disruptions hit with regularity and capabilities for water utilities to accommodate them change at a dizzying pace. Figure-it-out jobs are popping up nationwide, and employees are responding favorably. It's time to take this approach to water management and measure the results.

Keep Doing What's Right

We need to do everything we can to conserve more water in our home landscapes. By making conscious choices and implementing water-saving measures in our gardens, lawns, and outdoor spaces, we contribute directly to the larger effort of preserving a precious resource. Installing efficient irrigation systems with smart controllers and drip irrigation lines not only reduces water waste but sets an example for our communities. Through these small-yet-impactful changes, we demonstrate that every drop saved matters, illustrating that a collective commitment to water conservation begins with the individual actions we take to cultivate sustainable landscapes.

2

It All Starts with Soil Health

FOR PLANTS TO GROW WELL and look or produce their best, they require two necessary natural resources: soil and water. Understanding the composition of your soil is critical to ensuring your plants receive adequate moisture. Different types of soil impact soil's water-holding capacity, in turn directly affecting how you manage water and create irrigation schedules best for your landscape.

Mainly, we think of water moving down in the soil, say, after irrigation or a rain event. But water actually moves in all directions in soil. Downward movement is associated with gravity, but capillary action also moves water up in the soil. It occurs in beds of soil and also in plants, drawing moisture up from the roots and into leaves. It's hard to observe capillary action in soil or plants directly, but when a drop of water lands on a paper towel, it is easier to see how water is drawn from wetter to drier areas.

Water molecules stick to each other; this is known as "the cohesion force." When molecules adhere to a surface with a different composition, it's known as "the adhesion force." Finer-textured soils will always have greater water-holding capacity simply because there is more soil surface—fine particles of soil mean more molecules available for the water particles to adhere to. When lower soil layers have more moisture than the upper layers, capillary action draws water upward.

Soil particles have space between them. This space should ideally be shared by water and oxygen. When only water fills the space, plants are deprived of oxygen and will eventually die. Water runs in the spaces between soil particles; the larger the space between particles, the more water the soil can hold. It is essential to understand the soil type in your garden because there is a maximum amount of water a given type can hold. When you apply more water than the soil can hold, you're simply wasting water. The waste moves on from your intended watering zone in the form of runoff, or simply by moving past (and away from) the root zone of your plant.

Determining Your Soil Type

It is essential to identify the soil type, or types, in your landscape so you can adapt your watering practice to match the soil's ability to absorb the amount of water you apply.

Clay soils hold more water than other soils. Because water percolates slowly through clay soils, adhering to its many soil particles as it flows, water has the time to spread widely. Therefore, water penetrates clay soil slowly overall, and there are issues with soil runoff with clay soil more than other soils. In addition, while the ability of clay soils to hold water longer than other soils may seem like a benefit, the flip side is that the small pores inherent in clay soils don't allow air to be exchanged readily with the atmosphere, meaning it is often oxygen-deficient. Flooding clay soils with water leaves even less space for air. Clay soils should be watered slowly and infrequently.

Silty soils come between clay and sand, and include sediment including rock and mineral particles (often quartz) that are larger than clay but smaller than sand. These soils have moderate water retention and drainage. Silt soils retain moisture better than sandy soils, and provide water to plants more readily than clay soils.

Sandy soils absorb water more quickly than other soils, because the large pore spaces between the (relatively) large sand particles allow for flow. This also means the water does not move as widely across an area as it would with other soils. Sandy soils need to be watered for longer times and more frequently than clay soils.

Loamy soils are known as the best soil for gardeners. This is true because they contain both clay and sandy particles—the best of both worlds. The holding capacity and wetting pattern of clay soils combined with a better absorption rate and reasonable movement of water create a good mixture of water and oxygen in the soil.

Available Water Capacity by Soil Texture

Soil texture is the proportion of small, medium, and large particles (clay, silt, and sand, respectively) in a specific soil mass. For example, a coarse soil is a sand or loamy sand, a medium soil is a loam, silt loam, or silt, and a fine soil is a sandy clay, silty clay, or clay.

TEXTURE	INCHES OF WATER
Coarse sand	.25–.75
Fine sand	.75–1.00
Loamy sand	1.10–1.20
Sandy loam	1.25–1.40
Fine sandy loam	1.50–2.00
Silt loam	2.00–2.50
Silty clay loam	1.80–2.00
Silty loam	1.50–1.70
Clay	1.20–1.50

It's easy to see from this table that the type of soil you have impacts the amount of water it can hold. Taking time to evaluate soil structure helps us manage water in the garden. In addition, selecting the right plants for our gardens based on soil structure improves future maintenance and waste reduction.

Soil Testing

Knowing your soil type is critical to good water management and water savings. But how do you determine what type of soil you have? Performing either at least a basic home test or, preferably, sending out a sample for a scientific soil analysis, should be one of the first steps you take before planting anything in your home garden; if you've been gardening for several years and wonder about why your plants aren't as healthy as you'd like (or are dying), you can perform one at any time and then make a plan to amend your soil. Many of us never take this important first step, contributing to wasted resources and time. The U.S. Department of Agriculture recommends soil testing as an essential tool for finding out information on fertility and pH. Along with results, many scientific tests provide guidance about what amendments you should add to increase the productivity of your soil. Without a soil test, you may be spending money and wasting time by adding the wrong amendment, or too much of a specific nutrient.

What Is a Soil Test?

A soil test will tell you the composition of soil type in your landscape, and is a powerful tool to help you manage the mineral nutrition available to your growing plants, to help plants thrive. It is a quick and inexpensive way to check the levels of essential soil nutrients. It's also simple to complete: Take or send a sample of your soil to a nearby lab and have it tested. Local state university extension programs are a reliable resource, but there are many private environmental consultants and online soil-testing kits available as well.

The Hand Test

The simplest type of test is the hand test—the quickest, most straightforward way to evaluate your soil.

Simply scoop a handful of soil from your garden into your hand. Discard any obvious roots or large pebbles. Knead this in your hand to break down any compacted soil clumps.

Next, add a few drops of water to the soil until you can work it into a ball, ensuring the soil is evenly wet throughout. If the soil won't form a ball, you have sandy soil.

If the soil **does** form a ball, place it between your thumb and forefinger and squeeze it to create a ribbon. If the ribbon moves forward and the soil stays together, keep pressing it out until it eventually falls off. This is an indication of clay soil.

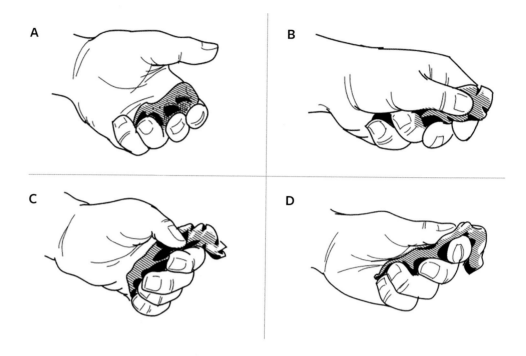

A

B

C

D

If you cannot get a ribbon out of the soil, but it did form a ball, you have a loamy sand soil.

The soil will also have a consistency that aligns with what the different types of material naturally feel like. Smear it around in the palm of your hand, then recheck the length of the ribbon against the chart below to determine the type of soil.

| | SIZE OF RIBBON | | |
	Less than 1" (2.5cm)	1–2" (2.5cm–5cm)	More than 2" (5cm)
GRITTY	Sandy loam	Sandy clay loam	Sandy clay
SMOOTH	Silty loam	Silty clay loam	Silty clay
STICKY	Loam	Clay loam	Clay

26

The Jar Test

The jar test is a home alternative to a lab test or a hand test.

1 Select a straight-sided jar and fill ⅓ of the jar with soil from the area you want to test. A 16-ounce jar should be large enough.

2 Add water until the jar is almost full.

3 Add one teaspoon of dish soap to the jar.

4 Shake the jar, then let the particles settle.

5 After a minute, measure and mark the sand depth. This will be the lightest color of particles, those that have settled at the bottom of the jar. They are the largest and heaviest.

6 Mark the silt depth after 6 hours.

7 At the 24-hour mark, mark the clay depth.

Jar Testing for Soil Type

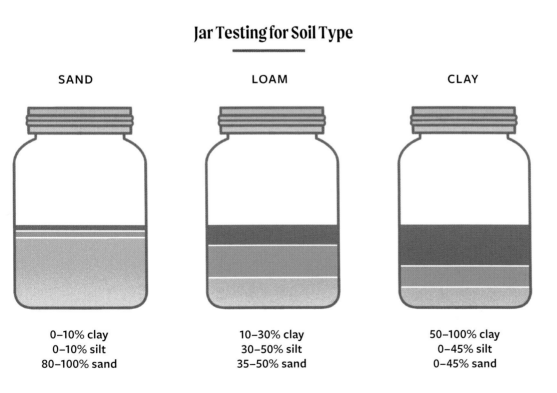

SAND	LOAM	CLAY
0–10% clay	10–30% clay	50–100% clay
0–10% silt	30–50% silt	0–45% silt
80–100% sand	35–50% sand	0–45% sand

8 Place a ruler next to the jar and measure the total height of the three layers. Then, measure the individual layers and determine the percentage of each.

  a Height of sand layer = _____ inches
  b Height of silt layer = _____ inches
  c Height of clay layer = _____ inches
  d % sand = sand height/total height x 100
  e % silt = silt height/total height x 100
  f % clay = clay height/total height x 100
  g Next, use the soil texture triangle to determine the makeup of the soil.

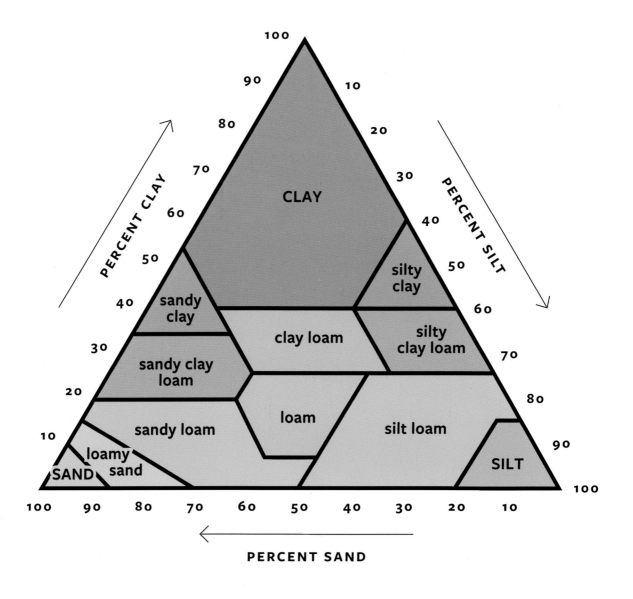

Laboratory Tests

Home tests are a great start to get a general idea of what type of soil you have, or if you don't have funds to arrange lab tests for every area of your garden you'd like to test. But it's a best practice to get a lab test of your soil if possible. The test provides insight into what you can't see just by looking at or feeling your soil. The information gained will remove a lot of guesswork from your planting plan. It offers valuable information pertaining to watering, and just as important, it identifies what nutrients the soil needs, so you save money by adding only the nutrients lacking, and by adding sufficient quantities from the start.

Soil test results contain:

1 Soil pH

2 The amount of potassium (K), phosphorus (P), calcium (Ca), magnesium (Mg) and sulfur (S)

3 The percentage of organic matter in your soil

4 How much lime and fertilizer (organic or chemical) are needed to optimize your soil

How do I take a soil sample for a lab?

Use a clean spade or shovel to dig a V-shaped hole 4 to 6 inches down into the soil. Cut a ½-inch slice of the dug-up soil—this is one sample. Take six to eight of these samples in each area of the garden where you'd like analysis performed. You can mix the samples from one area together.

An example of different areas where different tests would be useful might be from your vegetable garden, a lawn, a shrub area or border, or an annual color bed. These would all be considered separate "areas" and require separate samples since each type of planting growing there has different nutrient and water needs.

Label the samples appropriately and take them or ship them to a soil lab. Be sure you use a waterproof pen! Also, seal the bags so none of the separate areas' samples mix.

How much does a soil test cost?

This varies from lab to lab and depends on the amount of detailed information requested. For most home gardeners, a test will cost less than $50. It is a bargain considering the value of knowing exactly what your soil needs to grow a thriving garden and considering the cost of soil and amendments. You can find a soil lab by Googling soil tests, contacting your local Master Gardener Association, or contacting your local cooperative extension office. Once lab results are received, certain labs may also be willing to assist you in interpreting the data and recommending what is needed to improve the soil for your purposes.

Here is an example of a soil test on a property I manage. As you can see, the test makes fertilization recommendations as well.

Considering the reasonable expense of the test, the ease of taking samples, and the knowledge gained from the results, a soil sample should be at the top of every gardener and grower's list.

ANALYSIS RESULTS

Analysis	Result
Organic Matter, %	2.6
Phosphorous, ppm P (Cray-1 Equivalent)	57
Potassium, ppm K	139
Magnesium, ppm Mg	380
Calcium, ppm Ca	1400
Cation exchange capacity, meq/100g	10.7
pH	6.9

ANNUAL NUTRIENT REQUIREMENT

Pounds per 100 Square Feet					
Lime	Nitrogen (N)	Phosphorous (P2O5)	Potassium (K2O)	Magnesium (Mg)	Sulfur (S)
0	0.4	0.0	0.1	0.0	

SUGGESTED FERTILIZER APPLICATION

	NPK Fertilizer Grade	Description
Product	28-0-3	Slow Release N Fertilizer

COMMENTS

Use the fertilizer listed above or another material of similar NPK analysis. Split the recommended amount into at least 3 applications over the growing season. Apply ⅓ in the early spring, late spring, and early fall. Water well after each application.

Healthy soil is the key to more productive gardens and home landscapes. Soil health is also a pivotal contributor to proper water management. Soil delivers water and nutrients to crops, physically supports plants, helps control pests, determines where rainfall goes after it hits the earth, and protects the quality of drinking water, air, and wildlife habitat. Good soil management protects your soil, enhances performance, and preserves environmental quality for decades.

	Very Low	Low	Medium	High	Very High

Pounds per 1,000 Square Feet					
Lime	Nitrogen (N)	Phosphorous (P2O5)	Potassium (K2O)	Magnesium (Mg)	Sulfur (S)
0	4	0	1	0	

Annual Application Rate		
lbs per 100 sq. ft.		lbs per 100 sq. ft.
1.4	or	14.3
	or	

Next Steps: The Soil Percolation Test

Knowing the makeup of the soil in your garden helps to know how much water your soil can hold at any given time. Just as important, however, is to determine how well water penetrates the soil.

We consistently have to answer two questions:

1 How much we need to water.
2 How long we need to water.

A soil percolation test helps us decide how long to water.

Mature plants should receive the same amount of water during each irrigation session. The factor that changes is the frequency we need to water. Think about watering a mature lavender plant, for example. Lavender plants have a root depth of 8 to 10 inches. Say you've determined that this plant needs to receive half a gallon of water once a week. But if a scorching day comes along, you might decide to give it 2 gallons. What happens? The extra water will just move down past the root zone and be wasted. Each time you water, you want to soak the soil just to the point of its water-holding capacity for the root zone—no more and no less.

A percolation test helps us know how fast water moves in our soil so we don't water past the root zone. For water to move down in the soil, the water in the soil needs to be above "field capacity."

Basic Percolation Test:

1 Dig a hole 12 inches deep and about 12 inches wide. Make sure the sides are straight and the hole has a flat bottom.

2 Fill the hole with water to and let it drain completely. This "presoaks" the soil to ensure the water hits field capacity before you next measure the movement through the soil.

3 Place a ruler in the hole, or any measuring device where you can mark the water's depth, and again fill the hole with water.

4 Check how many inches the water level drops in the hole each hour. This provides the speed of water penetrating the soil.

Poorly draining soil will drop less than ½ inch per hour. The soil is considered to drain well if 1 to 2 inches of drainage is observed. If the water drops more than

3 inches an hour, the soil is too thirsty for success with home gardening, and must be amended.

Putting Test Results to Work in the Garden

Soil isn't just a static medium; it's a dynamic, living environment that constantly interacts with water. At the heart of this relationship lie four crucial points that determine water availability to plants and, in turn, profoundly impact water management practices.

Soil Saturation Point – This condition is when the soil holds only water, leaving no room for air. Plants can't live in this wet condition because they need oxygen, just like you and me. Think of it as a completely wet sponge, dripping

Soil Water Content

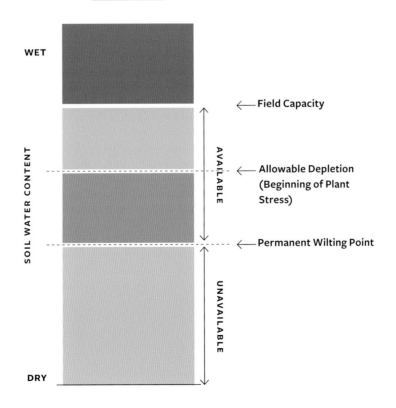

WET

SOIL WATER CONTENT

AVAILABLE

UNAVAILABLE

DRY

Field Capacity

Allowable Depletion
(Beginning of Plant
Stress)

Permanent Wilting Point

water as you lift it out of a bucket. Also, saturated soil is of course unable to absorb any additional water, so irrigating any more is a waste. Saturation often happens when we're hand watering. You may notice when soil reaches the saturation point, and the additional water runs off the soil's surface.

Field Capacity – This is the amount of soil moisture (water content) held in the soil after excess water drains. When soil is irrigated correctly, we reach this happy point of moistness. The soil has water and oxygen at field capacity, and both are readily available to the plants and soil microbes.

Permanent Wilting Point – This is when there is water in the soil, but the water is not available for plants, so the plants die. When a plant has been over-stressed consistently, it simply does not have enough energy to extract the water from the soil even if it's present. The capacity of the soil to hold on to the water is stronger than the plant's ability to extract the water. The difference in water content between field capacity and permanent wilting point is the amount of water available to plants.

Oven Dry – The opposite of saturated, oven dry occurs when there is no water in the soil whatsoever. Think of a sponge that has been left on the windowsill in the sun and turns crispy.

These basic tests and points reveal the complex balance between soil and water that underpins the success of any home water management strategy. Understanding them is paramount for sustainable use of water in our gardens and informed decision-making in the areas we need to irrigate in our home landscapes.

3

Predicting Plants' Daily Water Needs

WATER IS THE LIFEBLOOD OF OUR GARDENS, and gardeners must learn to manage water effectively to maintain a healthy and thriving landscape. Whereas commercial-scale growers often collect or have access to large data sets to track weather patterns and individual plant species' water needs, the home gardener too often is left to guess, based solely on the weather and personal observations of how the plants seem to look at the end of every day, all of course while working and attending to other life tasks and family needs. This results in inefficiency and water waste.

This is where taking a moment to formalize our observations by considering water use from a slightly new perspective—one that takes into account the role of basic evapotranspiration—can be transformative. This chapter defines evapotranspiration (ET), then helps gardeners grasp its basic effects on their plants and make appropriate changes to watering practices. Understanding a little bit about the science behind evapotranspiration and will help keep your garden thriving while conserving water.

How Plants Cycle Water

The easiest way to understand evapotranspiration is to consider it as the opposite of rain. Precipitation brings water into our landscape; evapotranspiration explains how water departs our landscape. To comprehend evapotranspiration fully, we need to break down this long word into its two components: "evaporation" and "transpiration."

Evaporation is the process by which water changes from liquid to vapor. It occurs on various surfaces, including soil, the surface of bodies of water, and even the leaves of plants. When the sun's energy heats these surfaces, it causes water to evaporate into the air.

Transpiration is a plant's version of sweating. Plants release water vapor from small openings in their leaves, called stomata. This release of water vapor into the

atmosphere is a crucial part of a plant's metabolism, if you will, facilitating the absorption of nutrients and helping to cool the plant down during hot weather.

It's difficult to observe transpiration with your eyes, but plants emit water almost all the time, to some degree. If you place a clear plastic bag around some leaves, before long you will observe water drops accumulating on the plastic.

Most plants' transpiration occurs during daylight hours. They still transpire at night, but at a significantly reduced rate. During a growing season, a leaf will transpire many times its weight in water. A large oak tree, for example, can transpire 40,000 gallons per year, or an average of 109 gallons per day.

Somewhere between 97% and 99% of the water a plant takes up through its roots will eventually pass out of the plant via evapotranspiration. Most of the water passes through the stomata on the leaves. Stomata are like donuts—round pores with a hole in the middle. The stomata open and close to regulate the amount of water leaving the plant. They are mostly found on the upper and lower surfaces of leaves, but occasionally they appear on stems, depending on the species of plant. Stomata also allow carbon dioxide in and oxygen out.

Factors that Influence Evapotranspiration Rates

Transpiration in plants is influenced by various factors, both environmental and plant-specific:

Temperature: Higher temperatures generally lead to increased transpiration rates. Warmer air in the atmosphere can hold more moisture, and since nature is always moving to balance elements, that simple chemical reaction drives water vapor loss from plant leaves.

Soil Moisture: What a plant senses about the moisture content of the soil can directly impact plant transpiration. A water-stressed plant may reduce transpiration to conserve water when the soil is dry. Conversely, well-watered plants are less likely to limit transpiration.

Plant Species: Different plant species have varying transpiration rates. For example, succulent plants, adapted to arid conditions, generally have lower transpiration rates than deciduous trees.

Leaf Surface Area: Plants with large leaf surfaces generally have high transpiration rates. More surface area means more stomata, therefore more potential for water loss.

Leaf Structure: Many leaves feature cuticles (an outermost protective layer) and/or trichomes (hairlike structures). Thicker cuticles and/or the presence of trichomes are both adaptations that can reduce water loss.

Plant Age: Young, rapidly growing plants often have higher transpiration rates than mature plants. As plants age and their growth slows, transpiration typically decreases.

Humidity: Lower humidity levels encourage faster transpiration because the difference in water vapor concentration between the leaf's interior and the surrounding air is significant. In humid conditions, transpiration slows down.

Light Intensity: Intense sunlight can stimulate transpiration, as it drives photosynthesis. When photosynthesis is happening, stomata open to allow carbon dioxide in, which also allows water vapor to escape.

Wind: Wind can pull water vapor away from a leaf's surface, effectively increasing the transpiration rate. Since it also increases air circulation around leaves, it reduces the humidity near the leaf surface, tempting water particles to move from areas of high concentration (on the leaf) to areas of low concentration (in the air).

CO_2 Concentration: Higher carbon dioxide levels in the air can reduce transpiration rates because plants can photosynthesize more efficiently in the presence of CO_2 with less stomatal opening.

Atmospheric Pressure: Changes in atmospheric pressure can influence transpiration rates, but this effect is typically minor compared to other factors.

These factors can often overlap, of course, and the specific impact of each factor can vary among plant species and in different environmental conditions. Gardeners and landscapers must note which of these factors might be affecting their local area when managing irrigation and caring for plants to optimize growth and conserve water.

The Watering Dilemma

Every gardener has been faced with the dilemma of how much and how often to water their plants. The answer lies in remembering to take evapotranspiration into consideration, especially when watering established plants.

The goal for watering is to give a plant the same amount each time—only the frequency of watering should change.

Water managers at commercial growing operations know how quickly water is lost from a landscape or garden because they monitor evapotranspiration. Home gardeners can do this on a smaller scale as well, to determine how much water your plants need to stay healthy without overwatering.

Measuring Evapotransporation at Home

Because different plants transpire water at different rates, one measurement of evapotranspiration (ET) cannot apply to all plants. For example, a succulent transpires water at a much lower rate than grass. So, scientists developed "reference evapotranspiration" rates instead of providing an ET reading for every plant. Home gardeners and landscapers can benefit from learning how their plants compare to reference evapotranspiration. Reference Evapotranspiration (ETo) is a standardized measurement of the rate at which water is lost from a well-watered, actively growing, and adequately maintained reference crop or surface under specific weather conditions. ETo is a baseline for estimating how much water is lost through evapotranspiration from other plants or surfaces in a given location.

ETo is typically expressed in units of length per day, such as inches per day (in/day). It represents the depth of water, in inches, that is needed to replace the moisture lost through evapotranspiration from a reference crop or plant. For example, say yesterday's ETo was .25 inches. This means .25 inches of water needs to be returned to the soil to replace the water that evaporated and transpired yesterday for the reference plant. However, one additional step needs to be taken. This step is knowing how your plants compare to the ETo example crop or plant.

In practical terms, reference ETo helps anyone managing water to make informed decisions about when to water their plants. By multiplying daily ETo by a specific plant's crop coefficient, irrigation schedules are matched to the plant's particular needs. Chapter 4 covers this in more detail. Know that it is important to understand, for example, that if you are watering roses with a crop coefficient of .7, the ETo of .25 has to be multiplied by .7 to get the water requirement for roses on that day.

ETo x crop coefficient = ET for the specific plant.

Actual formula: $ETo \times Kc = ETc$

The calculation for roses in the example above is .25 x .7 = .175 inches

Different plants have different water needs. Using crop coefficients, you can adjust the reference evapotranspiration to match the water requirements of your specific plants.

Evapotranspiration data is reported in several forms. The most common are historical ET and real-time ET. Real-time ET data is the best because it accurately reports the ET for the current day. Historical ET reports what is usually the average ET on a given day of the year. The advantage of using real-time ET data is that it gives you the opportunity to replace the water you know was lost on the previous day. Historical ET data also cannot capture important information like rain, clouds, and unusually high or low temperatures.

Some irrigation companies can now provide predictions for ET data up to six days into the future. This is very valuable, because if you know you will receive rain in the next few days, you may choose to irrigate less today.

ETo is a crucial parameter for irrigation management because it helps determine how much water crops require to grow optimally. For a more detailed exploration of using multiple atmospheric factors to calculate ET more accurately, see the Appendix.

Finding Evapotranspiration Data

Now that we know how to use ET data, the question turns to where home gardeners can obtain regular and reliable ET information. If you live in a rural city in the United States, often ET data is listed in the newspaper and sometimes reported on the radio. As you can imagine, this data is crucial daily information for growers.

A common way to obtain real-time ET data is from a small weather station. However, weather stations with capacity to calculate data are expensive (in the hundreds of dollars) and need regular maintenance, making them impractical for most home gardeners.

There are two practical ways to obtain ET data on a real-time basis. First, there are free services provided by various government agencies that offer real-time ET data from their weather stations.

A word of caution about ET data: it's important to find data that applies to your region and microclimate. Also, remember there is a period between when you receive your ET calculation and when you water. ET is still actively taking place during this time, so you must also replace the water that evaporates during that gap in time. For example, if you look up an ET reading at 8 a.m. and don't water until that evening, almost a full day of ET won't be accounted for in your calculation.

Government Agencies

The National Weather Service provides a map at https://www.weather.gov/ict/evapo-transpiration, one of its National Digital Forecast Database Graphical Forecasts,

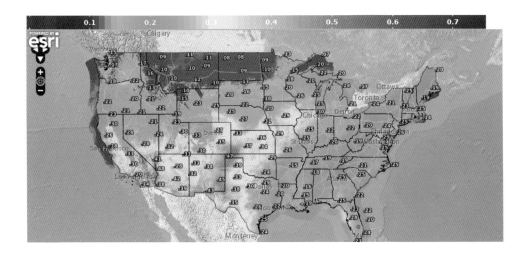

with a toggle menu that allow you to choose "Daily FRET (in)"—FRET stands for Forecast Reference EvapoTranspiration—and is zoomable to your locality. It looks like the chart on the previous page.

Many states also provide this ET information in similar formats. For example, California's Irrigation Management Information Service provides a map with a legend keyed to each region in the state, providing monthly average ETo numbers, useful particularly if checking ET numbers daily isn't practical for you. See the Resources section at the back of this book for a more complete list of state-by-state agencies that supply free ET data.

CALIFORNIA IRRIGATION MANAGEMENT INFORMATION SYSTEM (CIMIS)
REFERENCE EVAPOTRANSPIRATION ZONES

DEPARTMENT OF
WATER RESOURCES

UNIVERSITY OF
CALIFORNIA, DAVIS

STATE OF CALIFORNIA
ARNOLD SCHWARZENEGGER, GOVERNOR

DEPARTMENT OF WATER RESOURCES
LESTER A. SNOW, DIRECTOR

Lambert Conformal Conic Projection
1927 North American Datum

Reference EvapoTranspiration (ETo) Zones

1 **COASTAL PLAINS HEAVY FOG BELT** lowest ETo in California, characterized by dense fog

2 **COASTAL MIXED FOG AREA** less fog and higher ETo than zone 1

3 **COASTAL VALLEYS & PLAINS & NORTH COAST MOUNTAINS** more sunlight than zone 2

4 **SOUTH COAST INLAND PLAINS & MOUNTAINS NORTH OF SAN FRANCISCO** more sunlight and higher summer ETo than zone 3

5 **NORTHERN INLAND VALLEYS** valleys north of San Franciaco

6 **UPLAND CENTRAL COAST & LOS ANGELES BASIN** higher elevation coastal areas

7 **NORTHEASTERN PLAINS**

8 **INLAND SAN FRANCISCO BAY AREA** inland area near San Francisco with some marine influence

9 **SOUTH COAST MARINE TO DESERT TRANSITION** inland area between marine & desert climates

10 **NORTH CENTRAL PLATEAU & CENTRAL COAST RANGE** cool, high elevation areas with strong summer sunlight; zone has limited climate data & the zones selection is somewhat subjective

11 **CENTRAL SIERRA NEVADA** mountain valleys east of Sacramento with some influence from delta breeze in summer

12 **EAST SIDE SACRAMENTO-SAN JOAQUIN VALLEY** low winter & high summer ETo with slightly lower ETo than zone 14

13 **NORTHERN SIERRA NEVADA** northern Sierra Nevada mountain valleys with less marine influence than zone 11

14 **MID-CENTRAL VALLEY, SOUTHERN SIERRA NEVADA, TEHACHAPI & HIGH DESERT MOUNTAINS** high summer sunshine and wind in some locations

15 **NORTHERN & SOUTHERN SAN JOAQUIN VALLEY** slightly lower winter ETo due to fog and slightly higher summer ETo than zones 12 & 14

16 **WESTSIDE SAN JOAQUIN VALLEY & MOUNTAINS EAST & WEST OF IMPERIAL VALLEY**

17 **HIGH DESERT VALLEYS** valleys in the high desert near Nevada and Arizona

18 **IMPERIAL VALLEY, DEATH VALLEY & PALO VERDE** low desert areas with high sunlight & considerable heat advection

Monthly Average Reference Evapotranspiration by ETo Zone (inches/month)

Zone	Jan	Feb	Mar	Apr	May	Jun	Jul	Aug	Sep	Oct	Nov	Dec	Total
1	0.93	1.40	2.48	3.30	4.03	4.50	4.65	4.03	3.30	2.48	1.20	0.62	32.9
2	1.24	1.68	3.10	3.90	4.65	5.10	4.96	4.65	3.90	2.79	1.80	1.24	39.0
3	1.86	2.24	3.72	4.80	5.27	5.70	5.58	5.27	4.20	3.41	2.40	1.86	46.3
4	1.86	2.24	3.41	4.50	5.27	5.70	5.89	5.58	4.50	3.41	2.40	1.86	46.6
5	0.93	1.68	2.79	4.20	5.58	6.30	6.51	5.89	4.50	3.10	1.50	0.93	43.9
6	1.86	2.24	3.41	4.80	5.58	6.30	6.51	6.20	4.80	3.72	2.40	1.86	49.7
7	0.62	1.40	2.48	3.90	5.27	6.30	7.44	6.51	4.80	2.79	1.20	0.62	43.3
8	1.24	1.68	3.41	4.80	6.20	6.90	7.44	6.51	5.10	3.41	1.80	0.93	49.4
9	2.17	2.80	4.03	5.10	5.89	6.60	7.44	6.82	5.70	4.03	2.70	1.86	55.1
10	0.93	1.68	3.10	4.50	5.89	7.20	8.06	7.13	5.10	3.10	1.50	0.93	49.1
11	1.55	2.24	3.10	4.50	5.89	7.20	8.06	7.44	5.70	3.72	2.10	1.55	53.1
12	1.24	1.96	3.41	5.10	6.82	7.80	8.06	7.13	5.40	3.72	1.80	0.93	53.4
13	1.24	1.96	3.10	4.80	6.51	7.80	8.99	7.75	5.70	3.72	1.80	0.93	54.3
14	1.55	2.24	3.72	5.10	6.82	7.80	8.68	7.75	5.70	4.03	2.10	1.55	57.0
15	1.24	2.24	3.72	5.70	7.44	8.10	8.68	7.75	5.70	4.03	2.10	1.24	57.9
16	1.55	2.52	4.03	5.70	7.75	8.70	9.30	8.37	6.30	4.34	2.40	1.55	62.5
17	1.86	2.80	4.65	6.00	8.06	9.00	9.92	8.68	6.60	4.34	2.70	1.86	66.5
18	2.48	3.36	5.27	6.90	8.68	9.60	9.61	8.68	6.90	4.96	3.00	2.17	71.6

Variability between stations within single zones is as high as 0.02 inches per day for zone 1 and during winter months in zone 13. The average standard deviation of the ETo between estimation sites wihtin a zone for all months is about 0.01 inches per day for the 200 sites used to develop the map.

Smart Irrigation Controllers

Smart irrigation controllers can be an excellent way to adapt your watering schedule to ET, and are happily affordable for most homeowners, with widely available models ranging from $85 to $200. They often pay for themselves in one water billing cycle, as you adjust to water more efficiently. They tie in to the weather data from satellite observations and, via an app, allow you to customize timing for in-ground irrigation systems or adjust frequency based on real-time weather and forecasts. Many models also allow you to control which zone of your irrigation system to turn off or on with the app, so if water is rationed during high summer, say, you could opt to continue watering your vegetable garden but allow the lawn to go dormant.

For landscapers or homeowners with multiple acres to manage, it may be worth looking into the next level of smart irrigation tracking software, often available by subscription and based in the cloud, which can also predict daily irrigation costs based on your actual water bill. Over the years, several scientific models have been developed to estimate ET based on meteorological data. With these services, networks of ground-based weather stations provide real-time data on critical meteorological parameters such as temperature, humidity, solar radiation, and wind speed, essential inputs to ET estimation models. Some are simple empirical equations, while others are more complex and consider soil, plant, and atmospheric processes. The accuracy of ET predictions largely depends on the quality and relevance of the model used.

Pictured are screenshots from the dashboard of a Jain Unity smart controller. As you can see, it's easy to determine the daily ET requirements plus the prediction of ET for the next six days. This software also provides information on daily temperature and wind conditions, contributing to daily ET amounts.

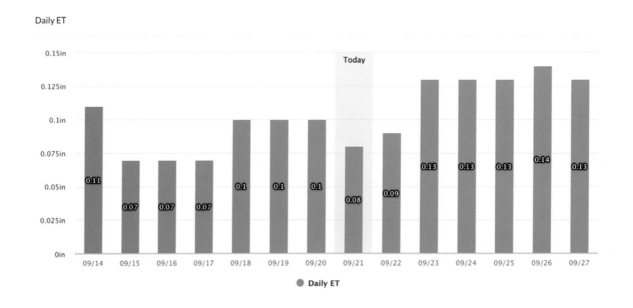

Wind Range

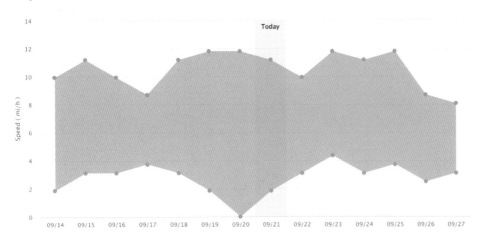

Temperature range

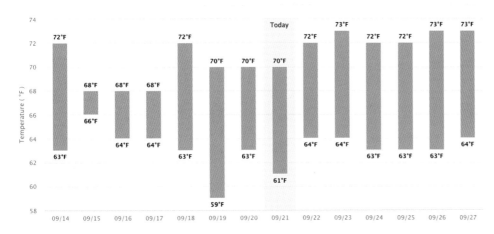

Modern ET estimation techniques often combine data from various sources (e.g., satellites, weather stations, soil moisture sensors) to improve accuracy. This multisource integration can provide a more comprehensive view of the factors influencing ET. With the advent of machine learning and the availability of vast datasets, it's now possible to refine ET prediction algorithms continually. Machine learning models can identify patterns and make more accurate predictions for future ET values by analyzing historical data.

The Penman-Monteith equation (see Appendix) is a widely used method for estimating reference evapotranspiration (ETo), which is the rate at which water is evaporated from a well-irrigated, uniform grass surface under specific weather conditions.

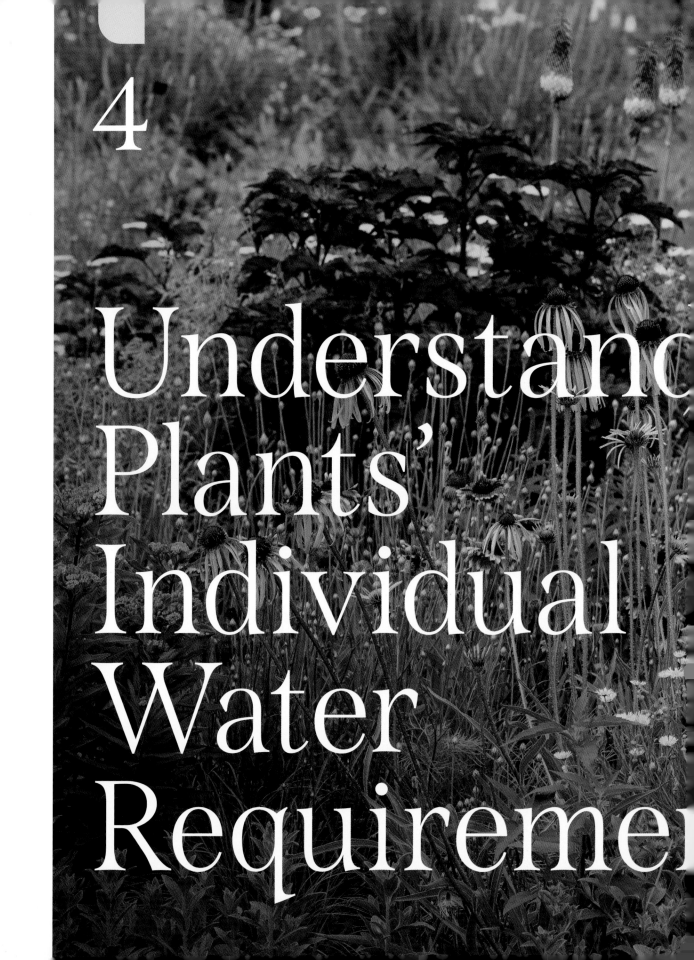

4

Understand
Plants'
Individual
Water
Requireme

WATER MANAGEMENT IS PARAMOUNT FOR our home landscapes and gardens, ensuring beauty and vigor while optimizing resource use. The professional irrigation industry has developed several tools and methodologies that can also be useful for home gardeners; they may seem technical at first, but they offer a comprehensive lens that will help us understand a plant's water needs depending on its specific species or type, ensuring irrigation practices that are both efficient and sustainable.

To help us plan yards that are waterwise, we can look at three factors: plant selection, and what the water-management industry calls "crop coefficients" and "WUCOLS" (Water Use Classification of Landscape Species, see page 56). These concepts, when combined, can form an important piece of effective home water management strategy.

In the last chapter, we covered evapotranspiration. One of the details discussed is that evapotranspiration rates are calculated based on a "reference crop," and given the symbol ETo. The farming terminology is the first clue that a reference crop will not typically be anything we grow on our landscapes or in our own gardens, however. So we need other ways to convert ETo into how much water to give the plants we typically have in our home gardens. We'll adopt terminology from commercial agriculture and call this a "crop coefficient." Looking at the combination of these two factors helps to estimate the water requirements of different plants at various stages of their growth. Here's how it's done.

Crop Coefficients

Crop coefficients (Kc) are used to relate the water use of a specific crop to the water use of a reference crop, typically grass or alfalfa. The process to determine these coefficients involves a combination of field research, instrumentation, and data analysis. Kc numbers adjust ETo to reflect the water needs of other specific crops or plants at specific stages of growth. These coefficients are developed from research and are typically provided in tables by plant. They can vary widely based on the plant type, its growth stage, and the local environment.

Here's a sample crop coefficient, for tomatoes:

CROP	KC INI	KC MID	KC END	ROOT DEPTH (INCHES)
tomato	0.7	1.05	0.8	12–36

Ini = early growth phase
Mid = mid-season, when the plant has leafed out fully
End = nearing the finish of the plant's life cycle

To find the actual water requirement of a specific plant (ET_c), you multiply the reference evapotranspiration (ET_o) by the crop coefficient (K_c) for that specific crop at its current growth stage: $ET_c = ET_o \times K_c$

For gardens and landscapes, especially those that are mixed with various plant species, determining an accurate crop coefficient can be more challenging than in a uniform agricultural setting where only one crop at a time is being considered. However, understanding and utilizing these coefficients can still be very beneficial and help us make practical decisions about watering levels at home.

At times it can be challenging to find specific information on plant water use. Crop coefficients are easily found for popular food crops like corn, tomatoes, squash, and cucumbers, which are often grown by large agricultural companies. The challenge is finding parallel information for the most popular home landscape plants. We can figure out appropriate watering levels, however, simply by multiplying crop coefficients, plant species factor (sometimes called plant factor, see page 53), and WUCOLS together.

Crop coefficients (K_c) can vary based on the age or growth stage of any plant. As plants grow and develop, their water needs change, so the crop coefficient adjusts to account for these variations at different stages over the plant's life cycle.

Here's a breakdown of how the crop coefficient typically varies with the growth stages:

Initial Stage: During the early growth phase, plants or crops have a small canopy, meaning less leaf surface area to transpire water. The crop coefficient during this stage is typically lower.

Crop Development Stage: As the plant grows and the canopy expands, its water demand increases. The crop coefficient rises during this phase and comes near to peaking.

Mid-Season or Full Cover Stage: At this stage, the plant or crop has reached its maximum canopy cover. The crop coefficient is at its highest because the crop is using the maximum amount of water for transpiration and cooling.

Late-Season or Maturity Stage: As the plant approaches maturity or begins to senesce, its water demand may decrease. The crop coefficient typically declines during this phase.

Applying Crop Coefficients to Home Gardens and Landscapes

While using crop coefficients for mixed gardens and landscapes involves a bit more personal observation about how your own garden is reacting to watering levels than might be required for large, uniform agricultural fields, the principle remains a valuable tool in estimating and managing water use efficiently.

Find Individual Plant Coefficients: Some horticultural and landscape research has provided crop coefficients for specific ornamental plants or trees. Start with a simple internet search for "crop coefficient" and your plant. Put this data to work if it's available for the species in your garden.

Group Plants by Water Needs: If you know the general water needs of the plants (e.g., low, medium, high), assign a general crop coefficient to those groups based on an average of several of the most prominent plants in that section of your garden.

Consult Local Experts: Nearby universities, agricultural extensions, or local water agencies might have researched and published crop coefficients specific to ornamental plants or trees native to or popular in your region.

Monitor Continuously: It's essential to monitor the landscape or garden for signs of health, vigor, and water stress. Adjust irrigation schedules based on plant robustness and seasonal changes.

Consider Local Variations: Microclimates, soil types, and specific garden conditions or weather extremes can influence the effectiveness of using crop coefficients. Always consider these local variations when applying Kc values.

Adjust with Experience: Over time, gardeners and landscapers learn to adjust the coefficients based on observations. If plants show signs of water stress, or if there's excessive water leading to runoff, the applied water and the assumed Kc might need adjustment.

Research has provided detailed crop coefficient curves for many prominent agricultural crops, showing how a Kc changes over the course of the growing season. These curves are particularly helpful for optimizing irrigation schedules to match the plant's actual water needs at different growth stages. It's worth noting that while the principle of changing water needs over growth stages applies to both agricultural crops and landscape plants, detailed Kc curves might not be readily available for all ornamental or landscape plants. In such cases, observations, making educated guesses based on similar data for like plants, experience, and consultation with local horticultural experts can help in estimating water needs over the plant's life cycle.

Plant Species Factor

The plant species factor, often referred to as "Ks" or "Kspecies," is a figure used to estimate the water requirement of specific plants or plant groups in the landscape. This reflects how a particular plant species's water use compares to that of a baseline reference plant, typically cool-season grass. Horticultural professionals determine a plant species factor by taking into account several considerations and research methodologies:

Field Studies: The most direct way to determine a plant species factor is through field studies. Researchers will measure the actual water use of a specific plant species over time and compare it to the water use of a reference plant (often cool-season grass).

Plant Origin and Habitat: Plants native to arid or semiarid regions typically have lower water requirements compared to those from wetter climates. The natural habitat of a plant species provides a basic understanding of its water needs.

Plant Physiology and Adaptations: Features such as waxy leaves, deep root systems, or the ability to go dormant during dry periods are adaptations that reduce water needs. Plants with such features might have a correspondingly lower plant species factor.

Growth Rate and Vigor: Fast-growing species might have higher water requirements than slow-growing or dormant ones.

Literature Review: Existing horticultural and botanical literature often contains information about the water needs of specific plant species. By reviewing these sources, researchers can gather data or make informed estimates about the species factor.

Expert Opinion: In the absence of direct research or clear literature, horticulturists, botanists, or landscape professionals familiar with local plant species might provide their expert opinions or observations on the relative water needs of plants.

Comparison to Known Species: If a particular species's water needs are unknown, it can be compared to a similar or related species with known water requirements.

Monitoring Plant Health: Over time, by observing plant health and vigor under different irrigation regimes, researchers or gardeners can deduce the relative water needs of a plant species. Stress symptoms, such as wilting or leaf drop, can indicate insufficient water.

Once a plant species factor is determined, it can be used in combination with other factors (like the evapotranspiration rate) to calculate the appropriate irrigation amount for that specific plant or group of plants in a landscape setting. It's worth noting that while tools like WUCOLS (see page 56) provide plant species factors for many landscape plants, such detailed resources might not be available everywhere, making local research and observation essential.

What Is the Difference between Crop Coefficients and Plant Species Factors?

Crop coefficients (Kc) and plant species factors (Ks) are both essential tools in irrigation planning, but they serve different purposes and are derived from different sources. Here's a breakdown of their differences:

Purpose and Application

Crop Coefficients (**Kc**): Kc values help determine the water requirements of specific crops at different growth stages. They're used to adjust the reference evapotranspiration (ETo) to estimate the actual evapotranspiration (ETc) of a particular crop, often an agricultural crop. In simple terms, Kc helps convert the water needs of a heavily studied baseline reference crop (usually grass or alfalfa) to the water needs of another specific plant.

 Plant Species Factors (**Ks**): More commonly used in landscaping and urban horticulture, Ks values indicate the water needs of various landscape plants compared to the reference ETo. They are particularly helpful in understanding how different landscape plants use water in comparison to the standard reference.

How It's Calculated

Kc: Derived from experimental data where the actual evapotranspiration (ETc) of a specific crop is measured and compared to the reference evapotranspiration (ETo). The ratio of ETc to ETo gives the Kc value.

 Ks: Typically derived from observational data and expert opinions based on how a specific landscape plant species performs under different watering regimes compared to the reference.

Variability

Kc: Changes with the growth stages of crops. For instance, a crop might have a different Kc value during its initial growth, mid-season, and at the end of its growth.

 Ks: Generally remains consistent for a given plant species in a particular region, although it might be adjusted based on specific conditions or plant varieties.

Usage Context

Kc: More detailed and often used for precision agriculture where water use optimization is critical for crop yield and quality.

 Ks: Used for broader landscape planning, where the goal is to maintain plant health and aesthetics rather than maximizing yield.

 In essence, while both Kc and Ks provide insights into plant water needs relative to a reference, Kc is more tailored to agriculture, and Ks is tailored to residential landscape plants and urban horticulture. Both play a crucial role in efficient water management in their respective contexts.

WUCOLS

WUCOLS, which stands for Water Use Classification of Landscape Species, is a resource created to provide guidance on the water needs of landscape species, and was developed and tailored specifically for California's diverse climates. The WUCOLS project classifies landscape plant species by their water needs in various regions of the state, but as California is of course a very large state with a wide range of climates, this data can be extrapolated for parallel wetter, drier, hotter, or cooler areas elsewhere country as well.

Plant Species Factor (Ks) and WUCOLS are both related to understanding the water requirements of plants, especially in landscaping. However, they are distinct in their focus and application:

WUCOLS classifies landscape plant species based on their water needs. It categorizes plants into different water use groups: Very Low, Low, Moderate, and High.

WUCOLS provides landscapers, gardeners, and water managers with a database of plants and their water needs, making it easier to select plants suitable for a region's water availability and to develop water-efficient landscapes.

WUCOLS was developed through a collaboration between the University of California Cooperative Extension, the California Department of Water Resources, and various other entities. It's particularly useful in areas where water conservation is crucial due to periodic droughts.

WUCOLS offers a comprehensive list of plants with ratings on their water usage, making it a go-to resource for plant selection based on water needs.

In summary, while the Plant Species Factor (Ks) is a numerical factor that adjusts the reference evapotranspiration for a specific plant's water needs, WUCOLS is a classification system and database that provides water use information for a wide range of landscape plants. The two can be used in conjunction, with Ks providing the quantitative adjustments and WUCOLS offering a broader categorization and selection tool.

There is nothing as comprehensive as WUCOLS outside of California. Some plant books and nurseries will say that a plant is a "low water use" or a "moderate water use" type, but that classification is a bit vague. Taking a WUCOLS rating from the closest regional match in California to your area can help you approximate the water use. It's too good of a resource not to use, even if you're adapting it to another state. As an example, you could use the WUCOLS values for Region 6 (Low Desert) to estimate the water use for plants in Phoenix, or Region 5 (High Desert) for Las Vegas. It gets a bit harder to translate as we move east, but given California's wide range of climates, we can get pretty close.

A word of warning about WUCOLS: It is in no way to be considered a scientific determination of actual water use. It is compiled from an anecdotal survey of landscape professionals based on their experiences. Then you need to consider the ranges of water use values applied to each water use category. "Low water use" is categorized as falling between 10% and 30% of ET. So a low water use plant could be one that uses .5 gallons per day of water . . . or three times that, 1.5 gallons per day. It's a rule of thumb more than a scientific pronouncement.

Where Can I Find Plant Water Requirement Information for My Specific Area?

Local Agricultural Extensions: Many regions have agricultural or cooperative extension services, often associated with land grant universities, that provide localized information on plant water needs and best irrigation practices.

Plant Databases: Some online databases or apps, such as the USDA's PLANTS Database, provide information about the native habitats of plants, which can give insights into their water requirements.

Local Nurseries and Botanical Gardens: Nurseries often provide care tags with plants that include watering needs, and nursery staff are often knowledgeable. Botanical gardens can also be a source of knowledge about local plants and their water requirements.

Irrigation Associations: Organizations such as the Irrigation Association in the U.S. offer resources and training materials regarding the water needs of landscape species in various regions.

Landscape Water Budgets: These are tools that calculate the appropriate amount of water for landscapes based on factors like plant water needs, local weather data, and soil type.

Landscape Professionals and Consultants: In areas without specific tools like WUCOLS, landscape architects, horticulturists, or irrigation consultants with experience in local plant species and climates can provide guidance on water management.

Research Publications: Scientific journals and research articles often have studies on water needs of specific plant species or plant groups in particular regions.

Regional Plant Lists: Some regions have developed lists of drought-tolerant or native plants tailored to local climates, which inherently consider water usage.

For websites offering these and additional resources, see the Appendix.

Water Use Tables for Popular Waterwise Plants, by Region

The following tables are meant to provide some trusted examples of popular plants by region that also happen to be waterwise, hopefully providing inspiration and options for home gardeners across the country. Each section lists ten or twenty plants that have proven to be resilient as well as beautiful, and which perform well in the listed region. Each region includes listings for shrubs, perennials, ground covers, and grasses—something for every area of your garden.

The root depth for shrubs can vary widely depending on the specific species, age, soil type, and other factors. The root depths provided are generalized. Also, for some plants, an exact depth might be more challenging to determine, so a range might be given. The crop coefficient values are also generalized and can vary based on the growth stage of the plant and other conditions. Likewise, WUCOLS classifications and plant species factors can vary depending on the specific species or cultivar and the location they are grown. Always refer to local and specific horticultural sources or research studies for more precise data when planning irrigation systems or setting up watering schedules.

This is a very general observation that helps with the concept of water use classifications for plants and a good start. As you move through the tables, they get more detailed.

By way of background, here are some baseline reference crops that have been heavily studied by the agricultural industry to establish crop coefficients (Kc) by growth cycle, and some of these may appear in your own home gardens as well of course.

CROP	KC INI	KC MID	KC END	ROOT DEPTH (INCHES)
alfalfa	0.4	1.2	1.15	36–96
apples	0.5	1.2	0.85	24–36
apricots	0.45	1.15	0.85	24–36
beans, green	0.5	1.05	0.9	24–36
beets	0.5	1.05	0.95	12–24
berries, bushes	0.3	1.05	0.5	12–36
broccoli	0.7	1.05	0.95	12–24
cabbage	0.7	1.05	0.95	12–24
cabbage-local	0.7	1.05	0.95	12–24
carrots	0.7	1.05	0.95	12–36
cauliflower	0.7	1.05	0.95	12–24
celery	0.7	1.05	0.95	12–24
cereal	0.3	1.15	0.25	24–48
cherries	0.5	1.2	0.85	24–36
cucumbers	0.6	1	0.75	6–12
grapes	0.3	0.8	0.5	36–72
green onions	0.7	1.05	0.95	6–12
lettuce	0.7	1	0.95	6–12
onions	0.7	1.05	0.95	12–24
pasture	0.4	1	0.85	24–72
peaches	0.45	1.15	0.85	24–36
pears	0.5	1.2	0.85	24–36
peas	0.5	1.15	1.1	12–24
potatoes	0.5	1.15	0.75	12–36
pumpkins	0.5	1	0.8	24–36
radishes	0.7	0.9	0.85	6–12
small vegetables	0.7	1.05	0.95	6–24
spinach	0.7	1.05	0.95	6–12

CROP	KC INI	KC MID	KC END	ROOT DEPTH (INCHES)
squashes	0.5	0.95	0.75	12–36
stone fruits	0.45	1.15	0.85	24–36
sweet corn	0.3	1.15	0.4	12–36
sweet peppers	0.7	1.05	0.85	12–24
tomatoes	0.7	1.05	0.8	12–36
tubers	0.5	1.05	0.95	12–36
watermelons	0.4	1	0.75	12–36

In general, the Ks for general categories of plants fall loosely into the following range, useful as a quick guide in case a plant you want to use isn't listed in one of the charts below.

Warm Season Turf, Irrigated	0.6	Bermuda, St. Augustine, Zoysia, Buffalo Grasses
Cool Season Turf, Irrigated	0.8	Fescue, Rye Grasses
Frequent Watering	0.8	Annual Flowers
Occasional Watering	0.5	Perennial Flowers, Ground Covers, Tender Woody Shrubs and Vines
Natural Rainfall	0.3	Tough Woody Shrubs and Vines and Non-Fruit Trees

The following regions of the country are represented in the following tables: Southern California, Northern California, the Pacific Northwest, the Desert Southwest, the Rockies, Texas, the Southeast, and the Northeast.

The Midwest and Great Plains states, comprising such a very large region of varied topography and climate, are not represented specifically. Readers from the Midwest and Great Plains are encouraged to compare their local climates to the charts on pages 44 and 45, and to search for parallel climatic conditions and guidance on WUCOLS and plant water requirement resources on pages 56 and 57, then browse the most similar featured regions for plants that would be suitable for your local home landscape.

Each featured region includes recommendations for waterwise shrubs, perennials, ground covers, and grasses.

Southern California

Waterwise Shrubs for Southern California

	COMMON NAME	SCIENTIFIC NAME	ESTIMATED KC VALUE	PLANT SPECIES FACTOR (KS)	WUCOLS CLASSIFICATION	ESTIMATED ROOT DEPTH (INCHES)
	BOUGAINVILLEA	Bougainvillea spp.	0.5–0.7	0.5–0.6	M	18–24
	CALIFORNIA LILAC	Ceanothus spp.	0.4–0.6	0.4–0.5	L	24–36
	COASTAL ROSEMARY	Westringia fruticosa	0.5–0.7	0.5–0.6	M	18–24
	INDIAN HAWTHORN	Rhaphiolepis indica	0.6–0.8	0.6–0.7	M	12–18
	INKBERRY	Ilex glabra	0.3–0.5	0.3–0.5	L	12–18
	LAVENDER	Lavandula spp.	0.4–0.6	0.3–0.4	L	12–18
	MANZANITA	Arctostaphylos spp.	0.3–0.5	0.3–0.4	L	24–36
	OLEANDER	Nerium oleander	0.7–0.9	0.7–0.8	M	24–36
	ROCKROSE	Cistus spp.	0.5–0.7	0.5–0.6	M	12–18
	TOYON	Heteromeles arbutifolia	0.5–0.7	0.5–0.6	M	18–24

Waterwise Perennials for Southern California

	COMMON NAME	SCIENTIFIC NAME	ESTIMATED KC VALUE	PLANT SPECIES FACTOR (KS)	WUCOLS CLASSIFICATION	ESTIMATED ROOT DEPTH (INCHES)
	AGAPANTHUS	Agapanthus spp.	0.6–0.8	0.7	M	18–24
	BLANKET FLOWER	Gaillardia grandiflora	0.5–0.7	0.6	M	12–18
	BUTTERFLY BUSH	Buddleia davidii	0.6–0.8	0.7	M	18–24
	CONEFLOWER	Echinacea purpurea	0.5–0.7	0.6	M	18–24
	CORAL BELLS	Heuchera spp.	0.5–0.6	0.5	M	12–18
	DAYLILY	Hemerocallis spp.	0.6–0.8	0.7	M	12–18
	FOXGLOVE	Digitalis purpurea	0.5–0.7	0.6	M	12–18
	GAURA	Gaura lindheimeri	0.6–0.7	0.6	M	18–24
	GERANIUM	Geranium spp.	0.5–0.7	0.6	M	12–18
	KANGAROO PAW	Anigozanthos spp.	0.5–0.7	0.6	L	12–18

COMMON NAME	SCIENTIFIC NAME	ESTIMATED KC VALUE	PLANT SPECIES FACTOR (KS)	WUCOLS CLASSIFICATION	ESTIMATED ROOT DEPTH (INCHES)
LAVENDER	Lavandula spp.	0.4–0.6	0.5	L	12–18
MEXICAN SAGE	Salvia leucantha	0.5–0.7	0.6	M	18–24
PENSTEMON	Penstemon spp.	0.5–0.7	0.6	L	12–18
RED HOT POKER	Kniphofia uvaria	0.6–0.7	0.7	M	18–24
RUSSIAN SAGE	Perovskia atriplicifolia	0.5–0.6	0.5	L	18–24
SALVIA	Salvia spp.	0.5–0.7	0.6	M	12–18
SHASTA DAISY	Leucanthemum x superbum	0.5–0.7	0.6	M	12–18
SOCIETY GARLIC	Tulbaghia violacea	0.5–0.6	0.5	M	12–18
VERBENA	Verbena spp.	0.5–0.7	0.6	M	12–18
YARROW	Achillea millefolium	0.5–0.7	0.6	L	12–18

UNDERSTANDING PLANTS' INDIVIDUAL WATER REQUIREMENTS

Waterwise Ground Covers for Southern California

	COMMON NAME	SCIENTIFIC NAME	ESTIMATED KC VALUE	PLANT SPECIES FACTOR (KS)	WUCOLS CLASSIFICATION	ESTIMATED ROOT DEPTH (INCHES)
	BLUE FESCUE	Festuca glauca	0.5–0.7	0.6	M	4–8
	BRASS BUTTONS	Leptinella squalida	0.5–0.6	0.6	M	2–4
	CANDYTUFT	Iberis sempervirens	0.5–0.7	0.6	M	4–8
	CARPET BUGLE	Ajuga reptans	0.6–0.8	0.7	M	4–8
	CORAL BELLS	Heuchera spp.	0.5–0.6	0.5	M	6–12
	CREEPING JENNY	Lysimachia nummularia	0.6–0.7	0.7	M	4–8
	CREEPING THYME	Thymus serpyllum	0.5–0.6	0.6	M	4–8
	DWARF PERIWINKLE	Vinca minor	0.6–0.8	0.7	M	6–12
	DYMONDIA	Dymondia margaretae	0.4–0.6	0.5	L	4–8
	ICE PLANT	Delosperma spp.	0.4–0.6	0.5	L	4–8

	COMMON NAME	SCIENTIFIC NAME	ESTIMATED KC VALUE	PLANT SPECIES FACTOR (KS)	WUCOLS CLASSIFICATION	ESTIMATED ROOT DEPTH (INCHES)
	KINNIKINNICK	Arctostaphylos uva-ursi	0.5–0.7	0.6	M	4–8
	LANTANA	Lantana montevidensis	0.5–0.7	0.6	M	4–8
	LILYTURF	Liriope muscari	0.6–0.8	0.7	M	4–8
	MONDO GRASS	Ophiopogon japonicus	0.6–0.8	0.7	M	4–8
	MYOPORUM	Myoporum parvifolium	0.5–0.7	0.6	M	6–12
	PROSTRATE ROSEMARY	Rosmarinus officinalis 'Prostratus'	0.5–0.7	0.6	M	6–12
	RED APPLE ICE PLANT	Aptenia cordifolia	0.5–0.6	0.6	M	4–8
	SEDUM (STONECROP)	Sedum spp.	0.4–0.6	0.5	L	4–8
	STAR JASMINE	Trachelospermum jasminoides	0.6–0.8	0.7	M	6–12
	STRAWBERRY CLOVER	Trifolium fragiferum	0.5–0.7	0.6	M	4–8

Waterwise Grasses for Southern California

	COMMON NAME	SCIENTIFIC NAME	ESTIMATED KC VALUE	PLANT SPECIES FACTOR (KS)	WUCOLS CLASSIFICATION	ESTIMATED ROOT DEPTH (INCHES)
	BERMUDA GRASS	Cynodon dactylon	0.6–0.8	0.7	M–H	6–12
	BLUE GRAMA	Bouteloua gracilis	0.4–0.6	0.5	L–M	4–8
	BUFFALO GRASS	Bouteloua dactyloides	0.4–0.6	0.5	L–M	4–8
	DEER GRASS	Muhlenbergia rigens	0.4–0.6	0.5	L	6–12
	FESCUE (TALL & FINE)	Festuca spp.	0.6–0.8	0.7	M	6–12
	KURAPIA (GROUND COVER)	Lippia nodiflora	0.6–0.7	0.6	M	4–8
	PASPALUM	Paspalum vaginatum	0.6–0.8	0.7	M	4–8
	RYEGRASS	Lolium spp.	0.7–0.9	0.8	H	4–8
	ST. AUGUSTINE GRASS	Stenotaphrum secundatum	0.7–0.9	0.8	H	6–12
	ZOYSIA GRASS	Zoysia spp.	0.6–0.8	0.7	M	6–12

Northern California

Waterwise Shrubs for Southern California

	COMMON NAME	SCIENTIFIC NAME	ESTIMATED KC VALUE	PLANT SPECIES FACTOR (KS)	WUCOLS CLASSIFICATION	ESTIMATED ROOT DEPTH (INCHES)
	BLUE ELDERBERRY	Sambucus nigra ssp. caerulea	0.5–0.7	0.6	M–H	18–36
	CALIFORNIA BUCKWHEAT	Eriogonum fasciculatum	0.3–0.5	0.4	L	18–36
	CALIFORNIA LILAC	Ceanothus 'Concha'	0.3–0.5	0.4	L	18–36
	CALIFORNIA SAGEBRUSH	Artemisia californica	0.3–0.5	0.4	L	12–24
	CEANOTHUS	Ceanothus spp.	0.3–0.5	0.4	L	18–48
	COFFEEBERRY	Rhamnus californica	0.3–0.5	0.4	L	18–36
	COYOTE BRUSH	Baccharis pilularis	0.4–0.6	0.5	L–M	18–36
	CURRANT	Ribes spp.	0.4–0.6	0.5	M	12–24
	MANZANITA	Arctostaphylos spp.	0.3–0.5	0.4	L	12–36

	COMMON NAME	SCIENTIFIC NAME	ESTIMATED KC VALUE	PLANT SPECIES FACTOR (KS)	WUCOLS CLASSIFICATION	ESTIMATED ROOT DEPTH (INCHES)
	MONKEY FLOWER	Mimulus spp.	0.4–0.6	0.5	M	12–24
	SPICEBUSH	Calycanthus occidentalis	0.5–0.7	0.6	M–H	12–24
	TOYON	Heteromeles arbutifolia	0.4–0.6	0.5	L–M	18–36
	TWINBERRY	Lonicera involucrata	0.5–0.7	0.6	M–H	18–36
	WAX MYRTLE	Myrica californica	0.5–0.7	0.6	M–H	18–36
	WESTERN REDBUD	Cercis occidentalis	0.4–0.6	0.5	M	12–24

Waterwise Perennials for Northern California

	COMMON NAME	SCIENTIFIC NAME	ESTIMATED KC VALUE	PLANT SPECIES FACTOR (KS)	WUCOLS CLASSIFICATION	ESTIMATED ROOT DEPTH (INCHES)
	BEE BALM	Monarda didyma	0.5–0.7	0.6	M	12–24
	BLACK–EYED SUSAN	Rudbeckia hirta	0.5–0.7	0.6	M	12–18
	BLEEDING HEART	Dicentra formosa	0.4–0.6	0.5	M	12–18
	CALIFORNIA FUCHSIA	Epilobium canum	0.3–0.5	0.4	L	12–24
	CATMINT	Nepeta spp.	0.4–0.6	0.5	L–M	12–18
	COLUMBINE	Aquilegia spp.	0.5–0.7	0.6	M	12–18
	CORAL BELLS	Heuchera spp.	0.5–0.7	0.6	M	12–18
	DAYLILY	Hemerocallis spp.	0.5–0.7	0.6	M	18–24
	ECHINACEA	Echinacea spp.	0.5–0.7	0.6	M	18–24
	FERNS (VARIOUS)	Polystichum spp.	0.4–0.6	0.5	L–M	12–18

	COMMON NAME	SCIENTIFIC NAME	ESTIMATED KC VALUE	PLANT SPECIES FACTOR (KS)	WUCOLS CLASSIFICATION	ESTIMATED ROOT DEPTH (INCHES)
	GOLDENROD	Solidago californica	0.4–0.6	0.5	L–M	18–24
	LAVENDER	Lavandula spp.	0.4–0.6	0.5	L	12–18
	LUPINE	Lupinus spp.	0.3–0.5	0.4	L	12–24
	MAIDEN GRASS	Miscanthus sinensis	0.5–0.7	0.6	M	18–36
	PENSTEMON	Penstemon spp.	0.4–0.6	0.5	L–M	12–18
	PHLOX	Phlox paniculata	0.5–0.7	0.6	M	12–18
	SALVIA	Salvia spp.	0.4–0.6	0.5	L–M	12–24
	SEDUM (STONECROP)	Sedum spp.	0.3–0.5	0.4	L	12–18
	SHASTA DAISY	Leucanthemum x superbum	0.5–0.7	0.6	M	12–18
	YARROW	Achillea millefolium	0.4–0.6	0.5	L	12–24

Waterwise Ground Covers for Northern California

	COMMON NAME	SCIENTIFIC NAME	ESTIMATED KC VALUE	PLANT SPECIES FACTOR (KS)	WUCOLS CLASSIFICATION	ESTIMATED ROOT DEPTH (INCHES)
	BLUE STAR CREEPER	Isotoma fluviatilis	0.4–0.6	0.5	L	3–6
	BRASS BUTTONS	Leptinella squalida	0.4–0.6	0.5	L	3–4
	CARPET BUGLE	Ajuga reptans	0.4–0.6	0.5	L	3–6
	CORAL BELLS	Heuchera spp.	0.5–0.7	0.6	M	12–18
	CREEPING JENNY	Lysimachia nummularia	0.4–0.6	0.5	L	2–4
	CREEPING THYME	Thymus serpyllum	0.3–0.5	0.4	L	3–6
	DWARF PERIWINKLE	Vinca minor	0.5–0.7	0.6	M	6 – 12
	IRISH MOSS	Sagina subulata	0.4–0.6	0.5	L	2–3
	KINNIKINNICK	Arctostaphylos uva–ursi	0.3–0.5	0.4	L	12–18
	LAMB'S EAR	Stachys byzantina	0.4–0.6	0.5	L	6–12

	COMMON NAME	SCIENTIFIC NAME	ESTIMATED KC VALUE	PLANT SPECIES FACTOR (KS)	WUCOLS CLASSIFICATION	ESTIMATED ROOT DEPTH (INCHES)
	MAZUS	Mazus reptans	0.4–0.6	0.5	L	2–4
	MONDO GRASS	Ophiopogon japonicus	0.5–0.7	0.6	M	6–8
	RED APPLE ICE PLANT	Aptenia cordifolia	0.4–0.6	0.5	L	4–6
	SEDUM (STONECROP)	Sedum spp.	0.3–0.5	0.4	L	4–6
	SNOW–IN– SUMMER	Cerastium tomentosum	0.4–0.6	0.5	L	6–8
	SWEET WOODRUFF	Galium odoratum	0.5–0.7	0.6	M	6–12
	TRAILING GAZANIA	Gazania rigens var. leucolaena	0.3–0.5	0.4	L	6–8

Waterwise Grasses for Northern California

	COMMON NAME	SCIENTIFIC NAME	ESTIMATED KC VALUE	PLANT SPECIES FACTOR (KS)	WUCOLS CLASSIFICATION	ESTIMATED ROOT DEPTH (INCHES)
	BENTGRASS	Agrostis spp.	0.7–0.9	0.8	M–H	6–12
	BLUE FESCUE	Festuca glauca	0.5–0.7	0.6	M	8–12
	BLUE GRAMA	Bouteloua gracilis	0.4–0.6	0.5	L	8–15
	BUFFALO GRASS	Bouteloua dactyloides	0.3–0.5	0.4	L	4–8
	CALIFORNIA FESCUE	Festuca californica	0.4–0.6	0.5	L	18–24
	CREEPING RED FESCUE	Festuca rubra	0.5–0.7	0.6	M	8–12
	DEER GRASS	Muhlenbergia rigens	0.4–0.6	0.5	L	24–36
	FINE FESCUE	Festuca spp.	0.5–0.7	0.6	M	6–12
	PURPLE NEEDLEGRASS	Nassella pulchra	0.3–0.5	0.4	L	24–36
	TALL FESCUE	Festuca arundinacea	0.6–0.8	0.7	M	12–30

The Pacific Northwest

Waterwise Shrubs for the Pacific Northwest

	COMMON NAME	SCIENTIFIC NAME	ESTIMATED KC VALUE	PLANT SPECIES FACTOR (KS)	WUCOLS CLASSIFICATION	ESTIMATED ROOT DEPTH (INCHES)
	DWARF OREGON GRAPE	Mahonia aquifolium	0.5–0.7	0.6	M	12–24
	EVERGREEN HUCKLEBERRY	Vaccinium ovatum	0.4–0.6	0.5	L	8–15
	NOOTKA ROSE	Rosa nutkana	0.6–0.8	0.7	M	12–24
	OREGON BOXWOOD	Pachysandra terminalis	0.4–0.6	0.5	L	6–12
	PACIFIC NINEBARK	Physocarpus capitatus	0.6–0.8	0.7	M	15–30
	RED OSIER DOGWOOD	Cornus sericea	0.6–0.8	0.7	M	15–30
	RED–FLOWERING CURRANT	Ribes sanguineum	0.5–0.7	0.6	M	12–18
	RHODODEN-DRON	Rhododendron spp.	0.5–0.7	0.6	M	12–18
	SALAL	Gaultheria shallon	0.5–0.7	0.6	M	10–20
	VINE MAPLE	Acer circinatum	0.5–0.7	0.6	M	15–25

Waterwise Perennials for the Pacific Northwest

	COMMON NAME	SCIENTIFIC NAME	ESTIMATED KC VALUE	PLANT SPECIES FACTOR (KS)	WUCOLS CLASSIFICATION	ESTIMATED ROOT DEPTH (INCHES)
	BLEEDING HEART	Dicentra formosa	0.6–0.8	0.7	M	8–12
	CAMAS	Camassia quamash	0.4–0.6	0.5	L	8–15
	COLUMBINE	Aquilegia formosa	0.5–0.7	0.6	M	8–15
	DOUGLAS ASTER	Aster subspicatus	0.6–0.8	0.7	M	10–20
	FAWN LILY	Erythronium oregonum	0.5–0.7	0.6	M	6–10
	FIREWEED	Chamerion angustifolium	0.6–0.8	0.7	M	12–24
	FOAM FLOWER	Tiarella trifoliata	0.5–0.7	0.6	M	6–12
	FRINGECUP	Tellima grandiflora	0.5–0.7	0.6	M	6–12
	GOLDENROD	Solidago canadensis	0.6–0.8	0.7	M	10–20
	LADY FERN	Athyrium filix–femina	0.5–0.7	0.6	M	8–15

Waterwise Perennials for the Pacific Northwest, *continued*

	COMMON NAME	SCIENTIFIC NAME	ESTIMATED KC VALUE	PLANT SPECIES FACTOR (KS)	WUCOLS CLASSIFICATION	ESTIMATED ROOT DEPTH (INCHES)
	MEADOW RUE	Thalictrum occidentale	0.5–0.7	0.6	M	12–18
	OX–EYE DAISY	Leucanthemum vulgare	0.6–0.8	0.7	M	8–15
	PENSTEMON	Penstemon spp.	0.5–0.7	0.6	M	10–20
	PIGGYBACK PLANT	Tolmiea menziesii	0.4–0.6	0.5	L	6–10
	RED HOT POKER	Kniphofia uvaria	0.6–0.8	0.7	M	12–24
	SHOOTING STAR	Dodecatheon hendersonii	0.5–0.7	0.6	M	6–12
	SWORD FERN	Polystichum munitum	0.5–0.7	0.6	M	12–24
	TIGER LILY	Lilium columbianum	0.5–0.7	0.6	M	8–15
	TWINFLOWER	Linnaea borealis	0.4–0.6	0.5	L	6–10

Waterwise Ground Covers for the Pacific Northwest

	COMMON NAME	SCIENTIFIC NAME	ESTIMATED KC	ESTIMATED KS	WUCOLS CLASSIFICATION	ESTIMATED ROOT DEPTH (INCHES)
	BERGENIA	Bergenia cordifolia	0.6	0.85	Medium	8–12
	BRASS BUTTONS	Leptinella squalida	0.6	0.85	Medium	2–4
	CANDYTUFT	Iberis sempervirens	0.6	0.85	Medium	6–9
	CARPET BUGLE	Ajuga reptans	0.6	0.85	Medium	6–8
	CREEPING JENNY	Lysimachia nummularia	0.7	0.9	Medium	2–4
	CREEPING THYME	Thymus serpyllum	0.5	0.8	Low	2–4
	DWARF PERIWINKLE	Vinca minor	0.7	0.9	Medium	4–6
	KINNIKINNICK	Arctostaphylos uva–ursi	0.5	0.8	Low	12–15
	LAMB'S EARS	Stachys byzantina	0.5	0.8	Low	6–8
	OREGON STONECROP	Sedum oreganum	0.4	0.75	Very Low	2–4

Waterwise Ground Covers for the Pacific Northwest, *continued*

	COMMON NAME	SCIENTIFIC NAME	ESTIMATED KC	ESTIMATED KS	WUCOLS CLASSIFICATION	ESTIMATED ROOT DEPTH (INCHES)
	RED CREEPING THYME	Thymus serpyllum coccineus	0.5	0.8	Low	2–4
	SNOW–IN– SUMMER	Cerastium tomentosum	0.5	0.8	Low	6–8
	SPOTTED DEADNETTLE	Lamium maculatum	0.7	0.9	Medium	2–4
	SWEET WOODRUFF	Galium odoratum	0.6	0.85	Medium	6–12
	WINTERGREEN	Gaultheria procumbens	0.6	0.85	Medium	6–9
	WOOD SORREL	Oxalis oregana	0.6	0.85	Medium	4–6
	YELLOW ARCHANGE	Lamium galeobdolon	0.7	0.9	Medium	4–6

Waterwise Grasses for the Pacific Northwest

	COMMON NAME	SCIENTIFIC NAME	ESTIMATED KC	KS	WUCOLS CLASSIFICATION	ESTIMATED ROOT DEPTH (INCHES)
	BLUE FESCUE	Festuca glauca	0.6	0.85	Medium	6–12
	FEATHER REED GRASS	Calamagrostis x acutiflora	0.7	0.9	Medium	12–24
	IDAHO FESCUE	Festuca idahoensis	0.5	0.8	Low	12–24
	MAIDEN GRASS	Miscanthus sinensis	0.7	0.9	Medium	12–24
	PRAIRIE DROPSEED	Sporobolus heterolepis	0.5	0.8	Low	18–24
	PURPLE MOOR GRASS	Molinia caerulea	0.7	0.9	Medium	12–18
	RIBBON GRASS	Phalaris arundinacea	0.7	0.9	Medium	12–24
	SWITCHGRASS	Panicum virgatum	0.6	0.85	Medium	24–36
	TUFTED HAIR GRASS	Deschampsia cespitosa	0.6	0.85	Medium	12–24
	WESTERN FESCUE	Festuca occidentalis	0.5	0.8	Low	12–24

The Desert Southwest

Waterwise Shrubs for the Desert Southwest

	COMMON NAME	SCIENTIFIC NAME	ESTIMATED KC	KS	WUCOLS CLASSIFICATION	ESTIMATED ROOT DEPTH (INCHES)
	APACHE PLUME	Fallugia paradoxa	0.5–0.7	0.6	L	15–20
	BAJA FAIRY DUSTER	Calliandra californica	0.5–0.7	0.6	L	12–18
	BRITTLEBUS	Encelia farinosa	0.5–0.7	0.6	L	8–12
	CHUPAROSA	Justicia californica	0.6–0.8	0.7	M	12–18
	DESERT LAVENDER	Condea emoryi	0.5–0.7	0.6	L	15–20
	DESERT MARIGOLD	Baileya multiradiata	0.5–0.7	0.6	L	8–12
	DESERT SAGE	Salvia dorrii	0.5–0.7	0.6	L	12–15
	FOUR WING SALTBUSH	Atriplex canescens	0.5–0.7	0.6	L	15–20
	JOJOBA	Simmondsia chinensis	0.6–0.8	0.7	M	12–18

COMMON NAME	SCIENTIFIC NAME	ESTIMATED KC	KS	WUCOLS CLASSIFICATION	ESTIMATED ROOT DEPTH (INCHES)
MORMON TEA	Ephedra nevadensis	0.5–0.7	0.6	L	10–15
OCOTILLO	Fouquieria splendens	0.5–0.7	0.6	L	20–30
TURPENTINE BUSH	Ericameria laricifolia	0.5–0.7	0.6	L	10–15
YELLOW BELLS	Tecoma stans	0.6–0.8	0.7	M	15–20

Waterwise Perennials for the Desert Southwest

COMMON NAME	SCIENTIFIC NAME	ESTIMATED KC	KS	WUCOLS CLASSIFICATION	ESTIMATED ROOT DEPTH (INCHES)
ARIZONA POPPY	Kallstroemia grandiflora	0.5–0.7	0.6	L	8–12
BLACKFOOT DAISY	Melampodium leucanthum	0.5–0.7	0.6	L	8–10
BLUE PALO VERDE	Parkinsonia florida	0.5–0.7	0.65	L	20–30
CHOCOLATE FLOWER	Berlandiera lyrata	0.5–0.7	0.6	L	12–15

Waterwise Perennials for the Desert Southwest, *continued*

	COMMON NAME	SCIENTIFIC NAME	ESTIMATED KC	KS	WUCOLS CLASSIFICATION	ESTIMATED ROOT DEPTH (INCHES)
	DESERT MILKWEED	Asclepias subulata	0.5–0.7	0.65	L	10–15
	DESERT SENNA	Senna armata	0.5–0.7	0.6	L	10–15
	DESERT SUNFLOWER	Geraea canescens	0.5–0.7	0.6	L	6–10
	DESERT WILLOW	Chilopsis linearis	0.6–0.8	0.7	M	20–25
	FIRECRACKER PENSTEMON	Penstemon eatonii	0.5–0.7	0.6	L	10–15
	GLOBE MALLOW	Sphaeralcea ambigua	0.5–0.7	0.65	L	10–15
	HUMMINGBIRD TRUMPET	Epilobium canum ssp. latifolium	0.6–0.8	0.7	M	10–14
	INDIAN BLANKET	Gaillardia pulchella	0.5–0.7	0.6	L	6–10
	MEXICAN EVENING PRIMROSE	Oenothera speciosa	0.6–0.8	0.7	M	8–12
	PARRY'S AGAVE	Agave parryi	0.4–0.6	0.5	L	15–24

Waterwise Ground Covers for the Desert Southwest

	COMMON NAME	SCIENTIFIC NAME	ESTIMATED KC	ESTIMATED KS	WUCOLS CLASSIFICATION	ESTIMATED ROOT DEPTH (INCHES)
	ANGELITA DAISY	Tetraneuris acaulis	0.4–0.6	0.5	L	6–10
	BAJA RUELLIA	Ruellia peninsularis	0.4–0.6	0.5	L	10–15
	BLUE ELF ALOE	Aloe 'Blue Elf'	0.4–0.6	0.5	L	10–12
	DAMIANITA	Chrysactinia mexicana	0.5–0.7	0.6	L	8–12
	DESERT ZINNIA	Zinnia acerosa	0.4–0.6	0.5	L	8–10
	DWARF MYRTLE	Myrtus communis 'Compacta'	0.5–0.7	0.6	L	12–15
	GAZANIA	Gazania rigens	0.5–0.7	0.6	L	8–10
	ICE PLANT	Delosperma spp.	0.5–0.7	0.6	L	6–8
	LANTANA	Lantana montevidensis	0.5–0.7	0.6	L	6–10
	PENSTEMON	Penstemon spp.	0.5–0.7	0.6	L	10–15

Waterwise Ground Covers for the Desert Southwest, *continued*

	COMMON NAME	SCIENTIFIC NAME	ESTIMATED KC	ESTIMATED KS	WUCOLS CLASSIFICATION	ESTIMATED ROOT DEPTH (INCHES)
	PERKY SUE	Hymenoxys scaposa	0.4–0.6	0.5	L	6–8
	RED SPIKE ICE PLANT	Cephalophyllum 'Red Spike'	0.5–0.7	0.6	L	6–10
	SANTA RITA PRICKLY PEAR	Opuntia santa-rita	0.5–0.7	0.6	L	10–20
	SOAP ALOE	Aloe maculata	0.4–0.6	0.5	L	10–12
	SOCIETY GARLIC	Tulbaghia violacea	0.5–0.7	0.6	L	8–12
	SEDUM (STONECROP)	Sedum spp.	0.5–0.7	0.6	L	4–8
	THYME	Thymus spp.	0.5–0.7	0.6	L	4–6
	TRAILING GAZANIA	Gazania linearis	0.5–0.7	0.6	L	6–8
	TRAILING LANTANA	Lantana sellowiana	0.5–0.7	0.6	L	6–10
	TRAILING ROSEMARY	Rosmarinus officinalis 'Prostratus'	0.5–0.7	0.6	L	8–12

Waterwise Grasses for the Desert Southwest

	COMMON NAME	SCIENTIFIC NAME	ESTIMATED KC	ESTIMATED KS	WUCOLS CLASSIFICATION	ESTIMATED ROOT DEPTH (INCHES)
	BLUE GRAMA	Bouteloua gracilis	0.5–0.7	0.6	L	8–12
	BERMUDA GRASS	Cynodon dactylon	0.6–0.8	0.7	M	4–6
	BUFFALO GRASS	Buchloe dactyloides	0.4–0.6	0.5	L	4–6
	DEER GRASS	Muhlenbergia rigens	0.5–0.7	0.6	L	18–24
	MEXICAN FEATHER GRASS	Stipa tenuissima	0.5–0.7	0.6	L	12–18
	PERIWINKLE	Vinca major	0.6–0.8	0.7	M	6–12
	PINK MUHLY GRASS	Muhlenbergia capillaris	0.5–0.7	0.6	L	12–18
	RED FOUNTAIN GRASS	Pennisetum setaceum 'Rubrum'	0.5–0.7	0.6	L	12–18
	SIDE OATS GRAMA	Bouteloua curtipendula	0.5–0.7	0.6	L	10–14
	SPOROBOLUS	Sporobolus wrightii	0.5–0.7	0.6	L	18–24

The Rockies

Waterwise Shrubs for the Rockies

	COMMON NAME	SCIENTIFIC NAME	ESTIMATED KC	ESTIMATED KS	WUCOLS CLASSIFICATION	ROOT DEPTH (INCHES)
	BITTERBRUSH	Purshia tridentata	0.4–0.6	0.5	L	10–15
	BLUE MIST SPIREA	Caryopteris x clandonensis	0.5–0.7	0.6	M	10–15
	CHOKECHERRY	Prunus virginiana	0.6–0.8	0.7	M	15–20
	FERNBUSH	Chamaebatiaria millefolium	0.4–0.6	0.5	L	10–15
	GAMBEL OAK	Quercus gambelii	0.6–0.8	0.7	M	15–20
	KINNIKINNICK	Arctostaphylos uva-ursi	0.4–0.6	0.5	L	12–18
	MAHONIA	Mahonia repens	0.5–0.7	0.6	M	10–15
	MORMON TEA	Ephedra viridis	0.4–0.6	0.5	L	10–15
	MOUNTAIN MAHOGANY	Cercocarpus montanus	0.4–0.6	0.5	L	12–18

	COMMON NAME	SCIENTIFIC NAME	ESTIMATED KC	ESTIMATED KS	WUCOLS CLASSIFICATION	ROOT DEPTH (INCHES)
	RED OSIER DOGWOOD	Cornus sericea	0.6–0.8	0.7	M	10–15
	ROCKY MOUNTAIN JUNIPER	Juniperus scopulorum	0.4–0.6	0.5	L	15–20
	SASKATOON SERVICEBERRY	Amelanchier alnifolia	0.6–0.8	0.7	M	12–18
	THREELEAF SUMAC	Rhus trilobata	0.5–0.7	0.6	M	10–15
	TWINBERRY HONEYSUCKLE	Lonicera involucrata	0.6–0.8	0.7	M	10–15
	WOODS' ROSE	Rosa woodsii	0.6–0.8	0.7	M	8–12

Waterwise Perennials for the Rockies

	COMMON NAME	SCIENTIFIC NAME	ESTIMATED KC	ESTIMATED KS	WUCOLS CLASSIFICATION	ROOT DEPTH (INCHES)
	BLANKET FLOWER	Gaillardia aristata	0.4–0.6	0.5	L	6–10
	BLUE FLAX	Linum lewisii	0.5–0.7	0.6	M	8–12
	COLUMBINE	Aquilegia caerulea	0.5–0.7	0.6	M	8–12
	CONEFLOWER	Echinacea purpurea	0.5–0.7	0.6	M	8–12
	CORAL BELLS	Heuchera sanguinea	0.5–0.7	0.6	M	8–10
	COREOPSIS	Coreopsis grandiflora	0.4–0.6	0.5	L	8–12
	FIREWEED	Epilobium angustifolium	0.6–0.8	0.7	M	8–12
	GOLDENROD	Solidago spp.	0.6–0.8	0.7	M	10–15
	LAVENDER	Lavandula angustifolia	0.4–0.6	0.5	L	8–12
	LUPINE	Lupinus spp.	0.5–0.7	0.6	M	10–12

	COMMON NAME	SCIENTIFIC NAME	ESTIMATED KC	ESTIMATED KS	WUCOLS CLASSIFICATION	ROOT DEPTH (INCHES)
	PASQUE FLOWER	Pulsatilla v ulgaris	0.4–0.6	0.5	L	6–10
	PENSTEMON	Penstemon spp.	0.4–0.6	0.5	L	8–12
	RED HOT POKER	Kniphofia uvaria	0.6–0.8	0.7	M	12–15
	RUSSIAN SAGE	Perovskia atriplicifolia	0.4–0.6	0.5	L	10–15
	SALVIA	Salvia nemorosa	0.4–0.6	0.5	L	8–12
	SEDUM (STONECROP)	Sedum spp.	0.4–0.6	0.5	L	6–10
	THYME	Thymus spp.	0.4–0.6	0.5	L	4–8
	YARROW	Achillea millefolium	0.4–0.6	0.5	L	10–12
	YELLOW SUNDROPS	Oenothera macrocarpa	0.5–0.7	0.6	M	6–10
	YUCCA	Yucca spp.	0.4–0.6	0.5	L	10–15

Waterwise Ground Covers for the Rockies

	COMMON NAME	SCIENTIFIC NAME	ESTIMATED KC	ESTIMATED KS	WUCOLS CLASSIFICATION	ROOT DEPTH (INCHES)
	BLUE FESCUE	Festuca glauca	0.5–0.7	0.6	M	6–10
	CARPET BUGLE	Ajuga reptans	0.5–0.7	0.6	M	3–6
	CREEPING JENNY	Lysimachia nummularia	0.6–0.8	0.7	M	2–4
	CREEPING THYME	Thymus praecox	0.4–0.6	0.5	L	2–4
	CREEPING RASPBERRY	Rubus pentalobus	0.5–0.7	0.6	M	3–5
	HEN AND CHICKS	Sempervivum tectorum	0.4–0.6	0.5	L	4–6
	KINNIKINNICK	Arctostaphylos uva–ursi	0.4–0.6	0.5	L	6–10
	LAMB'S EAR	Stachys byzantina	0.5–0.7	0.6	M	4–8
	MOSS PINK	Phlox subulata	0.4–0.6	0.5	L	3–6
	PUSSYTOES	Antennaria spp.	0.4–0.6	0.5	L	3–5

	COMMON NAME	SCIENTIFIC NAME	ESTIMATED KC	ESTIMATED KS	WUCOLS CLASSIFICATION	ROOT DEPTH (INCHES)
	SNOW-IN-SUMMER	Cerastium tomentosum	0.4–0.6	0.5	L	3–6
	SEDUM (STONECROP)	Sedum spp.	0.4–0.6	0.5	L	3–6
	TURKISH VERONICA	Veronica liwanensis	0.5–0.7	0.6	M	2–4
	VINCA	Vinca minor	0.5–0.7	0.6	M	4–6
	WINTER-CREEPER	Euonymus fortunei	0.6–0.8	0.7	M	4–8
	WOOLLY THYME	Thymus pseudolanuginosus	0.4–0.6	0.5	L	2–4
	WOOLLY YARROW	Achillea tomentosa	0.4–0.6	0.5	L	6–10
	YELLOW ARCHANGEL	Lamium galeobdolon	0.6–0.8	0.7	M	3–5
	ZINNIA	Zinnia spp.	0.6–0.8	0.7	M	6–8

UNDERSTANDING PLANTS' INDIVIDUAL WATER REQUIREMENTS

Waterwise Grasses for the Rockies

	COMMON NAME	SCIENTIFIC NAME	ESTIMATED KC	ESTIMATED KS	WUCOLS CLASSIFICATION	ROOT DEPTH (INCHES)
	BIG BLUESTEM	Andropogon gerardii	0.5–0.7	0.6	M	18–24
	BLUE GRAMA	Bouteloua gracilis	0.4–0.6	0.5	L	6–12
	BUFFALO GRASS	Buchloe dactyloides	0.4–0.5	0.45	L	4–6
	INDIAN GRASS	Sorghastrum nutans	0.5–0.7	0.6	M	18–24
	LITTLE BLUESTEM	Schizachyrium scoparium	0.4–0.6	0.5	L	12–18
	PRAIRIE DROPSEED	Sporobolus heterolepis	0.4–0.6	0.5	L	18–24
	SIDEOATS GRAMA	Bouteloua curtipendula	0.5–0.7	0.6	M	12–18
	SWITCHGRASS	Panicum virgatum	0.6–0.8	0.7	M	24–36
	WESTERN WHEATGRASS	Pascopyrum smithii	0.5–0.7	0.6	M	12–18
	WOOLLY SEDGE	Carex pellita	0.5–0.7	0.6	M	6–12

Texas

Waterwise Shrubs for Texas

	COMMON NAME	SCIENTIFIC NAME	ESTIMATED KC	ESTIMATED KS	WUCOLS CLASSIFICATION	ROOT DEPTH (INCHES)
	AGARITA	Mahonia trifoliolata	0.5–0.7	0.6	M	12–24
	BARBADOS CHERRY	Malpighia glabra	0.6–0.8	0.7	M	12–18
	BLACK DALEA	Dalea frutescens	0.4–0.6	0.5	L	12–24
	CENIZO	Leucophyllum frutescens	0.4–0.6	0.5	L	18–24
	CORALBERRY	Symphoricarpos orbiculatus	0.6–0.8	0.7	M	12–18
	FLAME ACANTHUS	Anisacanthus quadrifidus	0.6–0.8	0.7	M	12–18
	MOUNTAIN SAGE	Salvia regla	0.6–0.8	0.7	M	12–24
	POSSUMHAW	Ilex decidua	0.5–0.7	0.6	M	18–24
	RED YUCCA	Hesperaloe parviflora	0.3–0.5	0.4	L	12–24

Waterwise Shrubs for Texas, *continued*

	COMMON NAME	SCIENTIFIC NAME	ESTIMATED KC	ESTIMATED KS	WUCOLS CLASSIFICATION	ROOT DEPTH (INCHES)
	TEXAS SAGE	Leucophyllum candidum	0.4–0.6	0.5	L	12–24
	TURK'S CAP	Malvaviscus arboreus	0.6–0.8	0.7	M	12–24
	WAX MYRTLE	Morella cerifera	0.6–0.8	0.7	M	18–24
	YAUPON HOLLY	Ilex vomitoria	0.6–0.8	0.7	M	12–24
	YELLOW BELLS	Tecoma stans	0.6–0.8	0.7	M	12–24

Waterwise Perennials for Texas

	COMMON NAME	SCIENTIFIC NAME	ESTIMATED KC	ESTIMATED KS	WUCOLS CLASSIFICATION	ROOT DEPTH (INCHES)
	AUTUMN SAGE	Salvia greggii	0.6–0.8	0.7	M	12–18
	BLACK–EYED SUSAN	Rudbeckia hirta	0.6–0.8	0.7	M	12–18
	BLUEBONNET	Lupinus texensis	0.4–0.6	0.5	L	6–12
	CONEFLOWER	Echinacea purpurea	0.6–0.8	0.7	M	12–18
	COREOPSIS	Coreopsis grandiflora	0.6–0.8	0.7	M	12–18
	DAYLILY	Hemerocallis spp.	0.6–0.8	0.7	M	12–18
	FIREBUSH	Hamelia patens	0.6–0.8	0.7	M	12–18
	FOUR–NERVE DAISY	Tetraneuris scaposa	0.5–0.7	0.6	M	6–12
	GAURA	Gaura lindheimeri	0.5–0.7	0.6	M	12–24
	INDIAN BLANKET	Gaillardia pulchella	0.6–0.8	0.7	M	6–12

Waterwise Perennials for Texas, *continued*

	COMMON NAME	SCIENTIFIC NAME	ESTIMATED KC	ESTIMATED KS	WUCOLS CLASSIFICATION	ROOT DEPTH (INCHES)
	LANTANA	Lantana camara	0.6–0.8	0.7	M	12–18
	MEALY BLUE SAGE	Salvia farinacea	0.6–0.8	0.7	M	12–18
	MEXICAN HAT	Ratibida columnifera	0.5–0.7	0.6	M	12–18
	PENSTEMON	Penstemon spp.	0.5–0.7	0.6	M	12–18
	PLUMBAGO	Plumbago auriculata	0.6–0.8	0.7	M	12–18
	PRAIRIE VERBENA	Glandularia bipinnatifida	0.5–0.7	0.6	M	6–12
	PURPLE CONEFLOWER	Echinacea purpurea	0.6–0.8	0.7	M	12–18
	RED HOT POKER	Kniphofia uvaria	0.6–0.8	0.7	M	12–24
	RUELLIA	Ruellia simplex	0.6–0.8	0.7	M	12–18
	TURK'S CAP LILY	Lilium superbum	0.6–0.8	0.7	M	12–18

Waterwise Ground Covers for Texas

	COMMON NAME	SCIENTIFIC NAME	ESTIMATED KC	ESTIMATED KS	WUCOLS CLASSIFICATION	ROOT DEPTH (INCHES)
	ASIAN JASMINE	Trachelospermum asiaticum	0.6–0.8	0.7	M	12–18
	BLUE MISTFLOWER	Conoclinium coelestinum	0.6–0.8	0.7	M	6–12
	CEDAR SEDGE	Carex planostachys	0.5–0.7	0.6	M	6–12
	DICHONDRA	Dichondra argentea	0.5–0.7	0.6	L	4–6
	FROGFRUIT	Phyla nodiflora	0.5–0.7	0.6	L	4–6
	HORSEHERB	Calyptocarpus vialis	0.4–0.6	0.5	L	4–6
	INLAND SEA OATS	Chasmanthium latifolium	0.6–0.8	0.7	M	12–18
	PURPLE TRAILING LANTANA	Lantana montevidensis	0.6–0.8	0.7	M	6–12
	MONDO GRASS	Ophiopogon japonicus	0.6–0.8	0.7	M	6–12
	PIGEONBERRY	Rivina humilis	0.5–0.7	0.6	L	4–6

TEXAS

Waterwise Ground Covers for Texas, *continued*

	COMMON NAME	SCIENTIFIC NAME	ESTIMATED KC	ESTIMATED KS	WUCOLS CLASSIFICATION	ROOT DEPTH (INCHES)
	PURSLANE	Portulaca oleracea	0.5–0.7	0.6	L	4–6
	SILVER PONYFOOT	Dichondra argentea	0.4–0.6	0.5	L	4–6
	SNAKE HERB	Dyschoriste linearis	0.5–0.7	0.6	L	6–12
	SPREADING STONECROP	Sedum kamtschaticum	0.4–0.6	0.5	L	4–6
	STAR JASMINE	Trachelo-spermum jasminoides	0.6–0.8	0.7	M	12–18
	STRAWBERRY CLOVER	Trifolium fragiferum	0.6–0.8	0.7	M	6–12
	TURK'S CAP	Malvaviscus arboreus	0.6–0.8	0.7	M	12–18
	WINECUP	Callirhoe involucrata	0.6–0.8	0.7	M	6–12
	WOOLY STEMODIA	Stemodia lanata	0.4–0.6	0.5	L	4–6

Waterwise Grasses for Texas

	COMMON NAME	SCIENTIFIC NAME	ESTIMATED KC	ESTIMATED KS	WUCOLS CLASSIFICATION	ROOT DEPTH (INCHES)
	BERMUDA GRASS	Cynodon dactylon	0.6–0.8	0.7	M	4–6
	BUFFALO GRASS	Bouteloua dactyloides	0.4–0.6	0.5	L	4–6
	BLUE GRAMA	Bouteloua gracilis	0.4–0.6	0.5	L	6–12
	BIG MUHLY	Muhlenbergia lindheimeri	0.6–0.8	0.7	M	18–24
	LITTLE BLUESTEM	Schizachyrium scoparium	0.5–0.7	0.6	L	12–18
	SWITCHGRASS	Panicum virgatum	0.6–0.8	0.7	M	18–24
	SIDEOATS GRAMA	Bouteloua curtipendula	0.5–0.7	0.6	L	12–18
	PINK MUHLY GRASS	Muhlenbergia capillaris	0.6–0.8	0.7	M	12–18
	ST. AUGUSTINE GRASS	Stenotaphrum secundatum	0.7–0.9	0.8	H	4–6
	ZOYSIA GRASS	Zoysia spp.	0.6–0.8	0.7	M	4–6

The Southeast

Waterwise Shrubs for the Southeast

	COMMON NAME	SCIENTIFIC NAME	ESTIMATED KC	ESTIMATED KS	WUCOLS CLASSIFICATION	ROOT DEPTH (INCHES)
	AZALEA	Rhododendron spp.	0.6–0.8	0.7	M	12–18
	CAMELLIA	Camellia spp.	0.6–0.8	0.7	M	12–18
	CRAPE MYRTLE	Lagerstroemia indica	0.6–0.8	0.7	M	18–24
	GARDENIA	Gardenia jasminoides	0.6–0.8	0.7	M	12–18
	HOLLY	Ilex spp.	0.6–0.8	0.7	M	18–24
	HYDRANGEA	Hydrangea spp.	0.6–0.8	0.7	M	12–18
	INDIAN HAWTHORN	Rhaphiolepis indica	0.5–0.7	0.6	L	12–18
	INKBERRY	Ilex glabra	0.3–0.5	0.3–0.5	L	12–18
	LOROPETALUM	Loropetalum chinense	0.5–0.7	0.6	L	12–18

100

COMMON NAME	SCIENTIFIC NAME	ESTIMATED KC	ESTIMATED KS	WUCOLS CLASSIFICATION	ROOT DEPTH (INCHES)
NANDINA	Nandina domestica	0.5–0.7	0.6	L	12–18
ROSE OF SHARON	Hibiscus syriacus	0.6–0.8	0.7	M	18–24
SOUTHERN MAGNOLIA	Magnolia grandiflora	0.6–0.8	0.7	M	36–48
SPIREA	Spiraea spp.	0.6–0.8	0.7	M	12–18
VIBURNUM	Viburnum spp.	0.6–0.8	0.7	M	18–24
WITCH HAZEL	Hamamelis spp.	0.5–0.7	0.6	L	12–18

Waterwise Perennials for the Southeast

	COMMON NAME	SCIENTIFIC NAME	ESTIMATED KC	ESTIMATED KS	WUCOLS CLASSIFICATION	ROOT DEPTH (INCHES)
	ASTERS	Aster spp.	0.6–0.8	0.7	M	12–18
	BEE BALM	Monarda didyma	0.6–0.8	0.7	M	12–18
	BLACK-EYED SUSAN	Rudbeckia hirta	0.5–0.7	0.6	L	18–24
	BLANKET FLOWER	Gaillardia pulchella	0.4–0.6	0.5	L	6–12
	BUTTERFLY WEED	Asclepias tuberosa	0.4–0.6	0.5	L	18–24
	CARDINAL FLOWER	Lobelia cardinalis	0.6–0.8	0.7	M	12–18
	CONEFLOWER	Echinacea purpurea	0.5–0.7	0.6	L	18–24
	CORAL BELLS	Heuchera americana	0.6–0.8	0.7	M	12–18
	COREOPSIS	Coreopsis spp.	0.5–0.7	0.6	L	12–18
	DAYLILY	Hemerocallis spp.	0.6–0.8	0.7	M	18–24

	COMMON NAME	SCIENTIFIC NAME	ESTIMATED KC	ESTIMATED KS	WUCOLS CLASSIFICATION	ROOT DEPTH (INCHES)
	HOSTA	Hosta spp.	0.6–0.8	0.7	M	12–18
	JOE PYE WEED	Eutrochium purpureum	0.6–0.8	0.7	M	24–36
	LENTEN ROS	Helleborus orientalis	0.6–0.8	0.7	M	8–12
	LILYTURF	Liriope muscari	0.6–0.8	0.7	M	12–18
	PHLOX	Phlox paniculata	0.6–0.8	0.7	M	12–18
	RUSSIAN SAGE	Perovskia atriplicifolia	0.5–0.7	0.6	L	12–18
	SOLOMON'S SEAL	Polygonatum biflorum	0.5–0.7	0.6	L	12–18
	SPIDERWORT	Tradescantia virginiana	0.5–0.7	0.6	L	12–18
	STOKES' ASTER	Stokesia laevis	0.5–0.7	0.6	L	12–18
	YARROW	Achillea millefolium	0.4–0.6	0.5	L	12–18

UNDERSTANDING PLANTS' INDIVIDUAL WATER REQUIREMENTS

Waterwise Ground Covers for the Southeast

	COMMON NAME	SCIENTIFIC NAME	ESTIMATED KC	ESTIMATED KS	WUCOLS CLASSIFICATION	ROOT DEPTH (INCHES)
	ASIATIC JASMINE	Trachelosper-mum asiaticum	0.6–0.8	0.7	M	6–12
	CARPET BUGLE	Ajuga reptans	0.6–0.8	0.7	M	3–6
	CAST IRON PLANT	Aspidistra elatior	0.5–0.7	0.6	L	8–12
	CREEPING JENNY	Lysimachia nummularia	0.6–0.8	0.7	M	3–6
	CREEPING PHLOX	Phlox subulata	0.6–0.8	0.7	M	3–6
	CREEPING THYME	Thymus serpyllum	0.5–0.7	0.6	L	2–4
	DAYLILY	Hemerocallis spp.	0.6–0.8	0.7	M	12–18
	DWARF PERIWINKLE	Vinca minor	0.6–0.8	0.7	M	4–8
	ENGLISH IVY	Hedera helix	0.6–0.8	0.7	M	6–12
	LANTANA	Lantana camara	0.6–0.8	0.7	M	12–18

	COMMON NAME	SCIENTIFIC NAME	ESTIMATED KC	ESTIMATED KS	WUCOLS CLASSIFICATION	ROOT DEPTH (INCHES)
	LILYTURF	Liriope muscari	0.6–0.8	0.7	M	12–18
	MONDO GRASS	Ophiopogon japonicus	0.5–0.7	0.6	L	6–12
	OREGON BOXWOOD	Pachysandra terminalis	0.6–0.8	0.7	M	6–12
	SEDUM (STONECROP)	Sedum spp.	0.5–0.7	0.6	L	2–6
	ST. JOHN'S WORT	Hypericum calycinum	0.6–0.8	0.7	M	6–12
	SWEET WOODRUFF	Galium odoratum	0.5–0.7	0.6	L	3–6
	VERBENA	Verbena canadensis	0.6–0.8	0.7	M	6–12
	VIRGINIA CREEPER	Parthenocissus quinquefolia	0.6–0.8	0.7	M	12–18
	WINTER-CREEPER	Euonymus fortunei	0.6–0.8	0.7	M	6–12
	YARROW	Achillea millefolium	0.5–0.7	0.6	L	6–12

UNDERSTANDING PLANTS' INDIVIDUAL WATER REQUIREMENTS

Waterwise Grasses for the Southeast

	COMMON NAME	SCIENTIFIC NAME	ESTIMATED KC	ESTIMATED KS	WUCOLS CLASSIFICATION	ROOT DEPTH (INCHES)
	BAHIAGRASS	Paspalum notatum	0.6–0.8	0.7	L	24–36
	BERMUDAGRASS	Cynodon dactylon	0.6–0.8	0.7	M	12–18
	BLUE GRAMA	Bouteloua gracilis	0.5–0.7	0.6	L	12–18
	CENTIPEDE GRASS	Eremochloa ophiuroides	0.6–0.8	0.7	L	12–18
	FESCUE (TALL & FINE)	Festuca arundinacea	0.6–0.8	0.7	M	18–24
	PINK MUHLY GRASS	Muhlenbergia capillaris	0.5–0.7	0.6	L	18–24
	RYEGRASS	Lolium spp.	0.6–0.8	0.7	M	6–12
	SWITCHGRASS	Panicum virgatum	0.5–0.7	0.6	L	36–48
	ST. AUGUSTINE GRASS	Stenotaphrum secundatum	0.6–0.8	0.7	M	18–24
	ZOYSIA GRASS	Zoysia spp.	0.6–0.8	0.7	M	6–12

The Northeast

Waterwise Shrubs for the Northeast

	COMMON NAME	SCIENTIFIC NAME	ESTIMATED KC	ESTIMATED KS	WUCOLS CLASSIFICATION	ROOT DEPTH (INCHES)
	AZALEA	Rhododendron spp.	0.6–0.8	0.7	M	12–24
	BAYBERRY	Myrica pensylvanica	0.5–0.7	0.6	L	12–18
	BLUEBERRY	Vaccinium corymbosum	0.6–0.8	0.7	M	12–24
	BURNING BUSH	Euonymus alatus	0.6–0.8	0.7	M	12–24
	DOGWOOD	Cornus spp.	0.6–0.8	0.7	M	12–24
	FORSYTHIA	Forsythia x intermedia	0.6–0.8	0.7	M	12–24
	HYDRANGEA	Hydrangea spp.	0.6–0.8	0.7	M	12–24
	INKBERRY	Ilex glabra	0.3–0.5	0.3–0.5	L	12–18
	JUNIPER	Juniperus spp.	0.5–0.7	0.6	L	12–18

Waterwise Shrubs for the Northeast, *continued*

	COMMON NAME	SCIENTIFIC NAME	ESTIMATED KC	ESTIMATED KS	WUCOLS CLASSIFICATION	ROOT DEPTH (INCHES)
	LILAC	Syringa vulgaris	0.6–0.8	0.7	M	12–24
	MOUNTAIN LAUREL	Kalmia latifolia	0.6–0.8	0.7	M	12–24
	RHODODENDRON	Rhododendron spp.	0.6–0.8	0.7	M	12–24
	SPIREA	Spiraea spp.	0.6–0.8	0.7	M	12–24
	WITCH HAZEL	Hamamelis spp.	0.5–0.7	0.6	L	12–18
	YEW	Taxus spp.	0.6–0.8	0.7	M	12–24

Waterwise Perennials for the Northeast

	COMMON NAME	SCIENTIFIC NAME	ESTIMATED KC	ESTIMATED KS	WUCOLS CLASSIFICATION	ROOT DEPTH (INCHES)
	ASTER	Aster spp.	0.6–0.8	0.7	M	12–18
	BEE BALM	Monarda didyma	0.6–0.8	0.7	M	12–18
	BLACK–EYED SUSAN	Rudbeckia hirta	0.5–0.7	0.6	L	12–18
	BLEEDING HEART	Dicentra spectabilis	0.6–0.8	0.7	M	12–18
	CONEFLOWER	Echinacea purpurea	0.5–0.7	0.6	L	12–18
	CORAL BELLS	Heuchera spp.	0.6–0.8	0.7	M	12–18
	DAYLILY	Hemerocallis spp.	0.6–0.8	0.7	M	12–24
	FERNS (VARIOUS)	Polystichum spp., etc.	0.6–0.8	0.7	M	12–24
	GOLDENROD	Solidago spp.	0.5–0.7	0.6	L	12–18
	HOSTA	Hosta spp.	0.6–0.8	0.7	M	12–24

	COMMON NAME	SCIENTIFIC NAME	ESTIMATED KC	ESTIMATED KS	WUCOLS CLASSIFICATION	ROOT DEPTH (INCHES)
	IRIS	Iris spp.	0.6–0.8	0.7	M	12–18
	LAVENDER	Lavandula spp.	0.4–0.6	0.5	L	12–18
	LUPINE	Lupinus spp.	0.6–0.8	0.7	M	12–18
	PEONY	Paeonia spp.	0.6–0.8	0.7	M	12–24
	PHLOX	Phlox paniculata	0.6–0.8	0.7	M	12–18
	SALVIA	Salvia spp.	0.5–0.7	0.6	L	12–18
	SEDUM	Sedum spp.	0.4–0.6	0.5	L	6–12
	SHASTA DAISY	Leucanthemum x superbum	0.6–0.8	0.7	M	12–18
	TULIPS	Tulipa spp.	0.6–0.8	0.7	M	6–12
	YARROW	Achillea millefolium	0.5–0.7	0.6	L	12–18

Waterwise Ground Covers for the Northeast

	COMMON NAME	SCIENTIFIC NAME	ESTIMATED KC	ESTIMATED KS	WUCOLS CLASSIFICATION	ROOT DEPTH (INCHES)
	BARREN STRAWBERRY	Waldsteinia fragarioides	0.5–0.7	0.6	L	3–6
	BUGLEWEED	Ajuga genevensis	0.5–0.7	0.6	L	3–6
	CANADIAN WILD GINGER	Asarum canadense	0.6–0.8	0.7	M	3–6
	CARPET BUGLE	Ajuga reptans	0.5–0.7	0.6	L	3–6
	CREEPING JENNY	Lysimachia nummularia	0.6–0.8	0.7	M	2–4
	CREEPING PHLOX	Phlox subulata	0.6–0.8	0.7	M	3–6
	CREEPING THYME	Thymus serpyllum	0.5–0.7	0.6	L	2–4
	DWARF PERIWINKLE	Vinca minor	0.6–0.8	0.7	M	4–6
	JAPANESE PACHYSANDRA	Pachysandra terminalis	0.6–0.8	0.7	M	6–8
	KINNIKINNICK	Arctostaphylos uva–ursi	0.5–0.7	0.6	L	3–6

	COMMON NAME	SCIENTIFIC NAME	ESTIMATED KC	ESTIMATED KS	WUCOLS CLASSIFICATION	ROOT DEPTH (INCHES)
	LILY–OF–THE–VALLEY	Convallaria majalis	0.6–0.8	0.7	M	6–8
	MOSS (VAR.)	Various spp.	0.5–0.6	0.5	VL	0.5–2
	SNOW–IN–SUMMER	Cerastium tomentosum	0.5–0.7	0.6	L	3–6
	SWEET WOODRUFF	Galium odoratum	0.6–0.8	0.7	M	4–6
	VIRGINIA CREEPER	Parthenocissus quinquefolia	0.6–0.8	0.7	M	10–15
	WILD STONECROP	Sedum ternatum	0.5–0.7	0.6	L	3–6
	WINTER-CREEPER	Euonymus fortunei	0.6–0.8	0.7	M	3–6
	WOOLLY THYME	Thymus pseudolanuginosus	0.5–0.7	0.6	L	2–4
	YELLOW ARCHANGEL	Lamiastrum galeobdolon	0.6–0.8	0.7	M	3–6

Waterwise Grasses for the Northeast

	COMMON NAME	SCIENTIFIC NAME	ESTIMATED KC	ESTIMATED KS	WUCOLS CLASSIFICATION	ROOT DEPTH (INCHES)
	BIG BLUESTEM	Andropogon gerardii	0.6–0.8	0.7	M	18–24
	BLUE FESCUE	Festuca glauca	0.6–0.8	0.7	M	6–12
	BLUE GRAMA	Bouteloua gracilis	0.6–0.8	0.7	M	6–12
	BUFFALO GRASS	Buchloe dactyloides	0.5–0.7	0.6	L	3–5
	FESCUE (TALL & FINE)	Festuca arundinacea	0.6–0.8	0.7	M	12–15
	INDIAN GRASS	Sorghastrum nutans	0.6–0.8	0.7	M	18–24
	LITTLE BLUESTEM	Schizachyrium scoparium	0.6–0.8	0.7	M	15–20
	PRAIRIE DROPSEED	Sporobolus heterolepis	0.5–0.7	0.6	L	15–20
	SWITCHGRASS	Panicum virgatum	0.6–0.8	0.7	M	18–24
	ZOYSIA GRASS	Zoysia spp.	0.6–0.8	0.7	M	6–8

The Author's Overall Favorites

A Combination of Beauty and Moderate Water Use

Research to see whether these could work for your region or zone. Trusted favorites!

	COMMON NAME	SCIENTIFIC NAME	ESTIMATED KC	ESTIMATED KS	WUCOLS CLASSIFICATION	ROOT DEPTH (INCHES)
	BOXWOOD	Buxus sempervirens	0.6–0.8	0.7	M	12–15
	DAHLIAS	Dahlia spp.	0.6–0.8	0.7	M	8–12
	DWARF MOUNTAIN PINE	Pinus mugo	0.6–0.8	0.7	M	20–24
	HEATHER	Calluna vulgaris	0.5–0.7	0.6	L	8–12
	LAMB'S EAR	Stachys byzantina	0.5–0.7	0.6	L	4–6
	LAVENDER	Lavandula spp.	0.2–0.4	0.4	L	8–12
	LEMON TREES	Citrus limon	0.7–0.9	0.8	MH	24–36
	LIME TREES	Citrus aurantiifolia	0.7–0.9	0.8	MH	24–36
	OLIVE TREES	Olea europaea	0.2–0.6	0.6	L	30–40

	COMMON NAME	SCIENTIFIC NAME	ESTIMATED KC	ESTIMATED KS	WUCOLS CLASSIFICATION	ROOT DEPTH (INCHES)
	ROSEMARY	Rosmarinus officinalis	0.2–0.6	0.6	L	8–12
	SANTA BARBARA DAISIES	Erigeron karvinskianus	0.2–0.6	0.6	L	6–8
	SAGE	Salvia spp.	0.2–0.6	0.6	L	10–14
	THYME	Thymus spp.	0.2–0.7	0.6	L	4–6
	YARROW	Achillea millefolium	0.2–0.7	0.6	L	10–14

5

How Often and How Long to Water

NOW, WITH THE SOLID GRASP OF evapotranspiration and an understanding of how to use crop coefficients, plant species factors, or WUCOLS covered by previous chapters, you can appreciate how the intricacies of soil texture relate to water holding capacity. This knowledge is all prerequisite to devising an irrigation schedule. Putting plants on a schedule informed by facts and science will ensure that they receive water precisely when they need it, optimizing the health and vigor of your landscape.

Water the Same Amount at Each Watering

For most mature plants, the best practice is to water them the same amount each time you water. The only thing that should change is the frequency of how often you water. Why? Each time you water, the goal should be to fill the soil to its water-holding capacity for your plant's root zone. No more and no less.

The first time you're trying to determine ideal soil water capacity, you'll need to monitor it as explained in the section on performing a soil percolation test in Chapter 2. Once you know how long your particular soil holds a given amount of water, you can determine when it reaches an allowable depletion level and refill it until it reaches max water holding capacity again. This consistent moisture will keep plants happiest. The principle of consistent volume application combined with variable frequency equals highly efficient irrigation. Then program your sprinkler or drip system to dispense the precise amount of water sufficient to replenish the soil profile to its "field capacity"—the maximum amount of water it can hold. This technique ensures that each watering session deeply saturates the soil.

By tailoring the watering schedule to the dynamic needs of the garden—not varying the volume—based on seasonal weather patterns, plant life cycles, and soil type, we can strike a delicate balance between plant health and water conservation. During cooler or rainy periods, reduce the frequency of watering. In the heat of summer, increase it. This method prevents both under-watering and over-watering, conserving water by ensuring that irrigation only occurs when necessary and that each drop can be used effectively by the plant to support plant life.

In practice, this approach translates to setting up your irrigation system to run for the same duration each time it is activated while adjusting the interval between watering sessions according to the current environmental conditions. A consistent-volume, variable-frequency watering strategy is a conscious step toward sustainable gardening, safeguarding our precious water resources while nurturing a vibrant and healthy garden ecosystem.

Watering Device Efficiency

Here are some approximate measures of watering devices, expressed in DU:

Spray heads – 50%
Rotors – 70%
Rotation nozzles – 72%
Drip irrigation – 90%
Point-source drip emitters – 93%

The type of emission device used makes a big difference in terms of how much water is wasted.

Creating a Watering Schedule

Several key factors go into determining a proper watering schedule. The first factor is called distribution uniformity, or DU. It sounds like a fancy term, but really it's just a way to measure how evenly water is distributed across a given area during irrigation/watering. There are two key reasons why DU matters for our home watering efforts.

Distribution Uniformity (DU)

First, DU tells us how much water reaches the plants' root zone compared to how much water is being applied to the bed the plants live in. The DU is usually expressed as a percentage—a higher percentage indicates more uniform water distribution. For example, most spray head irrigation mechanisms have low distribution uniformity. Many fall in the 50% range. This means 50% of the water you are paying for does not even get to your plants. Spray heads are used mostly to water lawns. When you hear people say take out the turf because it wastes water, what they should really be saying is take out the spray head irrigation because it wastes water. Where does the other 50% of the water go that doesn't make it to the roots? Most of it just evaporates before it hits the ground or is blown away by wind.

Second, for optimal plant health and growth, plants need a consistent amount of water. Each square foot in every planting bed should receive the same amount of water. If the irrigation system is not distributing water in a uniform way, some plants are being overwatered to get even a little water to the plants in the area of low distribution uniformity.

For example, if there are eight spray heads in a zone and six of the spray heads have a distribution uniformity of 50% and two have a distribution uniformity of 40%, water use should be calculated for all eight sprinklers according to the weakest link, or in this case the lowest distribution, 40%—or the plants in the area with 40% would not get enough water. The result is that most plants will be overwatered. This is wasteful and expensive.

Example of Good DU

Application depth ↗

Example of Poor DU

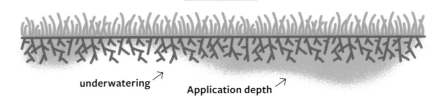

underwatering ↗　　Application depth ↗

Additional reasons for working to achieve high distribution uniformity with the irrigation system besides saving water and money are plentiful. For plants to thrive, they need a consistent amount of water. If one area receives too much water (over-irrigation) while another gets too little (under-irrigation), it can lead to uneven growth, stress, and potential plant loss.

Water applied too quickly or unevenly will often just become runoff. As it flows away, it will very likely carry away valuable topsoil, fertilizers, and pesticides with it, potentially causing environmental issues and reducing soil fertility. Uniform water distribution, on the other hand, ensures that fertilizers and nutrients

Help! Run times on my controller are listed in minutes, but my emission devices use measurements in gallons per hour! How do I convert this?

The discrepancy between evapotranspiration (ET) values quoted in inches and the irrigation output given in gallons per minute or per hour by many watering devices can pose a challenge for gardeners just looking to figure out how much to water their plants. However, there's a straightforward way to bridge this gap: converting the gallons per minute or per hour to inches of water. Here's how you can go about it:

1 Determine the Area Being Irrigated

Before you start, you'll need to know the size of the area that your emitter or sprinkler covers. This can be calculated in square feet (sq. ft) or square meters (sq. m), depending on your preference.

2 Convert the Emission Rate

Once you know the emission rate (in gallons per minute or hour) and the area it covers, you can calculate the depth of water being applied over that area in a given time. Here's the basic formula for converting gallons per hour (GPH) to inches:

$$\text{Inches per hour (IPH)} = \frac{\text{Gallons per hour (GPH)}}{\text{Area (sq. ft.)}} \times 0.623$$

3 Compare with ET Values

Once you've converted the emission rate to inches per hour (IPH) or per day, you can directly compare it with the ET values. This will allow you to determine if your irrigation system is supplying more, less, or the right amount of water compared to what the plants are losing through ET.

EXAMPLE:

Let's say you have a drip emitter that emits water at 1.0 gallons per hour and covers an area of 1 sq. ft.

$$IPH = \frac{1\ GPH}{1\ sq.\ ft.} \times 0.623$$

IPH= 1 × .623 = .623 inches per hour.

Let's say you have a sprinkler that emits water at 1.5 gallons per minute and covers an area of 100 sq. ft.

1.5 gpm = 90 gallons per hour

$$IPH = \frac{90\ GPH}{100\ sq.\ ft.} \times 0.623$$

IPH= .01 × .623 = .56

Next the inches per hour (IPH) have to be multiplied by the distribution uniformity (DU). Once you make this calculation, you'll start to see why drip emitters are better for conservation.

Take the .623 inches per hour for drip emitter and multiply this by the known distribution uniformity number for that device, in this case .90, and you get .56 inches per hour.

For the second example, take the .56 inches per hour for the spray head and multiply this by the distribution uniformity number for spray heads of .5. You get .28 inches per hour.

As this simple math shows us, you'd have to run the spray heads almost twice as long as the drip emitter to get the same amount of water delivered to the root zone for this area.

By converting the manufacturer's emission rates from gallons to inches, you can tailor your irrigation schedule to the actual water needs of the plants, as indicated by the ET values. This not only ensures optimal plant growth but also promotes water conservation by preventing overwatering.

will also be evenly distributed and will stay where they're meant to be absorbed. This means that plants across the landscape have equal access to the nutrients they need to grow.

An irrigation system with high DU will also generally require less frequent adjustments or repairs, saving both time and money.

Achieving good DU ensures that plants remain healthy, resources are used efficiently, and costs are kept in check. Properly managing DU can make a significant difference in the appearance, health, and sustainability of a garden or landscape.

Precipitation Rate

Part of watering is thinking about how quickly water is applied to any given area. Irrigation industry folks call this "precipitation rate." Home gardeners can think about it very much in terms of the most familiar precipitation: rainfall. Is it raining heavily, or is it barely sprinkling? How quickly water falls on an area affects how well it can be absorbed.

Precipitation rate is usually expressed in inches per hour (in/hr) or millimeters per hour (mm/hr). You've probably heard a local weatherman predict that it would rain 2 inches an hour on your local newscast, for example. Same thing. This rate is crucial for designing and managing your home irrigation system to ensure that water is applied evenly and efficiently, without overwatering or underwatering the plants.

Here's a more detailed explanation:

Definition: Precipitation rate is the rate at which an irrigation system distributes water over a specific area. It essentially defines how fast the irrigation system is "raining" on the plants.

Importance: Understanding the precipitation rate helps in matching the irrigation to the soil's absorption rate and the plants' water needs. If the rate is too high, water may run off or pool, rather than soaking into the soil. If it's too low, plants may not receive enough water.

Application Efficiency

Application efficiency refers to the measure of how effectively an irrigation system delivers water to the intended area and how well that water is used by the crops or plants. It's an important concept in both agricultural and home landscape irrigation for evaluating the performance of an irrigation system and ensuring water conservation. Here's a detailed explanation:

Definition: Application efficiency is the percentage of water applied that is actually used by the plants. It compares the amount of water that reaches the root zone of the plants to the total amount of water that has been applied by an irrigation system.

Factors Affecting Efficiency: Various factors can impact application efficiency, including:

- *System Design and Maintenance:* Poorly designed or maintained systems can lead to uneven water distribution.

- *Type of Irrigation System:* Drip irrigation systems generally have higher application efficiencies compared to sprinkler systems, as they deliver water directly to the plant's root zone.

- *Soil Type and Condition:* Water infiltration rates vary with different soil types, affecting how much water is actually made available to plants.

- *Water Pressure and Application Rate:* Incorrect pressure or application rates can lead to runoff or insufficient watering.

- *Environmental Conditions:* Wind, temperature, and humidity can affect how much water is lost to evaporation.

Importance: High application efficiency is crucial for conserving water, reducing costs, and ensuring optimal plant growth. It's especially important in areas of water scarcity.

Improvement Strategies: Application efficiency can be improved by:

- Regularly maintaining and adjusting irrigation systems.

- Using irrigation methods that match the needs of the plants and the local environment.

- Education on proper irrigation techniques and scheduling.

Additional Variables to Consider When Watering

1 What type of plant are you watering? Broadleaf? Succulent?

2 Irrigation method: spray, drip, rotor?

3 Maturity: newly planted, or established plantings?

4 What is your system's precipitation rate?

5 Are you getting good distribution uniformity?

6 Root depth: Do your plants have deep tap roots, or fairly shallow root balls?

7 Is your yard sloped, causing water to run down and pool?

8 How much sun or shade does your yard receive?

Application efficiency is a key metric in irrigation management, representing how well an irrigation system delivers water to plants and minimizing water loss. Improving application efficiency is essential for sustainable water use and effective irrigation practices.

Basic Irrigation Calculations

With those parameters in hand, you're now ready to make your own watering schedule calculation. Here's the basic formula:

T = Run time in minutes
ETo = Evapotransporation rate, in inches
Kc = Crop coefficient, percent
Pr = Precipitation rate of the area, in inches per hour
Ea = Application efficiency of the sprinkler system, percent
60 = Constant for conversion of area, flow, inches per hour, and inches per day into common units.

$$T = \frac{60 \times ETo \times Kc}{Pr \times Ea}$$

To practice, try using the following numbers in your calculation. These represent a typical turf irrigation calculation for a warm, not hot, climate:

Eto = 1 inch for the week
Kc = .8
Pr = .56
Ea = 50

$$T = \frac{60 \times 1 \times .8}{.56 \times .50}$$

Answer = water 171 minutes for the week.

Now let's perform the same calculation with drip irrigation:

ETo = 1 inch for the week
Kc = .8
Pr = 1
Ea = .90

$$T = \frac{60 \times 1 \times .8}{1 \times .90}$$

Calculation = water 53 minutes for the week.

What are the key differences between the two calculations? The only items that change are the precipitation rate (Pr) and the application efficiency (Ea). You can see immediately from the results how much moke efficient a drip irrigation system is over a sprinkler system.

Once you've made your total calculation of how many minutes to water over the course of a full week, your next decision to is think about how to divide that across seven days. You could run all the minutes one time per week, at once, or split it up over several consecutive days. How to judge?

Determining how many days to water per week and subsequently dividing your calculated total run time for irrigation is a decision that hinges on several factors related to your specific irrigation needs and environmental conditions. Here are the key considerations:

Soil Type: The soil's ability to hold water is a significant factor. Sandy soils drain quickly and may require more frequent watering, in shorter bursts. Clay soils, which hold water longer, can be watered less frequently but for longer periods of time in each watering session.

Plant Type: Different plants have different water requirements. Deep-rooted plants may prefer infrequent but deep watering, while shallow-rooted plants may need more frequent watering.

Climate and Weather Conditions: Hotter, drier climates typically necessitate more frequent watering. Conversely, in cooler or more humid climates, you may need to water less often. Also, consider the current weather patterns—if it's been raining over several days, you may need to water less.

Irrigation System Efficiency: Drip systems, which deliver water directly to the plant's roots, may allow for less frequent watering compared to sprinkler systems, which lose more water to evaporation.

Watering Restrictions: Be aware of any local watering restrictions or guidelines that might dictate specific watering days, such as regulations requiring addresses ending in even or odd numbers to only water on even or odd days, or outright bans on landscape water usage in the heat of summer.

Watering Deeply and Infrequently: This approach encourages deeper root growth, which is beneficial for plant health. Over-watering or too-frequent watering can lead to plants developing shallow root systems, which in turn potentially increases water waste because they're unable to absorb water lower in soil.

Observation and Adjustment: Start with a schedule based on your best calculations and estimate considering the factors above, but always remember to simply observe your plants. Signs of under-watering include wilting or yellowing leaves. Adjust your schedule based on plant health and soil moisture.

To begin, start with a basic division of the total watering time by the number of days you plan to water. Consider for this example the total run time is 60 minutes per week:

If you think it's best to water once a week, run the system for the full 60 minutes in one session.

If you think your garden would do best if watered three times a week, divide 60 minutes by 3, resulting in 20 minutes per session. Remember, these are just starting points. You'll need to observe your garden's response and adjust accordingly. It's often beneficial to start with less frequent, longer watering sessions to encourage deeper root growth and then adjust based on how your plants and soil respond. For most gardens and landscapes, only watering once a week might stress the plants. In addition, if your watering device puts out a lot of water, realize that much of the water will run past the root zone. Most of the time it is best to divide the total needed watering minutes across a few days.

Dividing the Total Run Time

Once you've determined the optimal frequency of watering (say twice a week, or every other day), divide your total weekly run time by the number of watering days. For instance, if your total run time is 210 minutes per week and you decide to water three times a week, you would water for 70 minutes each of those days.

In essence, the number of days you choose to water each week should be based on a combination of environmental conditions, plant needs, soil type, and practical considerations. It's often a balance between ensuring adequate hydration for your plants and promoting water conservation. Regular monitoring and adjustments are key to finding the right schedule for your specific situation.

There is also another, slightly more complicated calculation for this, in case you are interested in breaking out that calculator again. This is calculation takes into account the soil type, its water-holding capacity, and the water needs of the plants. This method is more precise, as it considers how quickly the soil can absorb water without causing runoff or wastage and ensures that plants receive adequate moisture down to the tips of their roots. Here's a basic overview of how this calculation is typically done:

Determine Soil Type: Identify your soil type (sandy, loamy, clay, etc.), as different soils have different water-holding capacities. For instance, sandy soil drains quickly and holds less water, while clay soil drains slowly and holds more water.

Calculate Available Water Capacity (AWC): AWC is the amount of water that the soil can hold and is available to plants. It's typically measured in inches of water per foot of soil. This varies by soil type:

- *Sandy soil* has an AWC of about 1 inch per foot.

- *Loamy soil* has an AWC of about 2 inches per foot.

- *Clay soil* has an AWC of about 2.5 inches per foot.

Determine Root Zone Depth: Know the effective root zone depth of your plants. Different plants' roots reach different depths. A little online research will probably give you a good estimate.

Calculate Total Available Water (TAW): Multiply the AWC by the root zone depth. This gives you the total amount of water your soil can hold for your plants.

Determine Management Allowed Depletion (MAD): This is the fraction of TAW that you allow to be depleted before irrigating again. It's often set at 50% for many crops, to prevent stress.

Advanced Irrigation Calculation:

First, calculate the Plant Available Water (PAW) by multiplying TAW with MAD. Then, monitor your soil moisture or use weather data to estimate how much water is used by the plants (evapotranspiration) and how much is added (by rainfall). When the available water in the soil is reduced to the PAW level, it's time to irrigate again.

Irrigation Amount: The amount of water to apply is the difference between the TAW and the current soil moisture level.

This method requires more data and often needs soil moisture monitoring equipment or tools for measuring evapotranspiration. It's a more tailored approach and takes more concentration and effort than the basic calculation, but it can significantly improve water use efficiency, especially for large gardens or homes with landscapes that cover several acres.

Calculating run times for irrigation scheduling requires effort and time—but it's always worth that effort, in dollars. It also offers numerous benefits that enhance both the efficiency and effectiveness of your watering practices. Here are the key advantages of doing these calculations:

Water Efficiency: Precise run times ensure that you're providing just the right amount of water—not too much, not too little. This minimizes water waste, which is especially important in areas with water scarcity or enforced restrictions.

Improved Plant Health: Proper irrigation scheduling helps in delivering the optimal amount of water to plants, which is crucial for their health and growth. Overwatering can lead to root rot or fungal diseases, while under-watering can stress plants, reducing their growth and yield.

Soil Preservation: Correct watering prevents soil erosion and nutrient runoff caused by excessive watering. It also helps maintain soil structure and aeration, which are vital for root health.

Cost Savings: Efficient water use leads to lower water bills. In large-scale agricultural settings, this can translate to substantial cost savings.

Environmental Responsibility: By avoiding overwatering, you reduce the leaching of fertilizers and chemicals into groundwater, thus protecting the environment.

Adaptability to Changing Conditions: With a calculated irrigation schedule, you can quickly adjust to changes in weather conditions, soil moisture levels, and plant needs, ensuring adaptability and resilience in your gardening or farming practices.

Maximizing Yield: In agricultural settings or vegetable gardens, proper watering can lead to better crop yields and quality, which is crucial for profitability.

Data-Driven Decisions: Using calculations and soil moisture sensors, if you can, for scheduling allows you to make informed, data-driven decisions rather than relying on guesswork.

Conservation of Resources: Efficient use of water is not only good for your wallet but also for the broader ecosystem, conserving water resources for future use and other needs.

Taking the time to calculate precise run times for irrigation scheduling is a smart investment in the health of your plants, the efficiency of your water use, and the overall sustainability of your gardening or farming practices.

If it feels overwhelming to make these calculations regularly, the next chapter is for you. (In this case, regularly means weekly. Some of the best water managers I know are only able to make this calculation monthly.) Smart controllers can make these calculations for you and adjust run times on a daily basis based on daily evapotranspiration data. This is by far the best way to go for most home water managers.

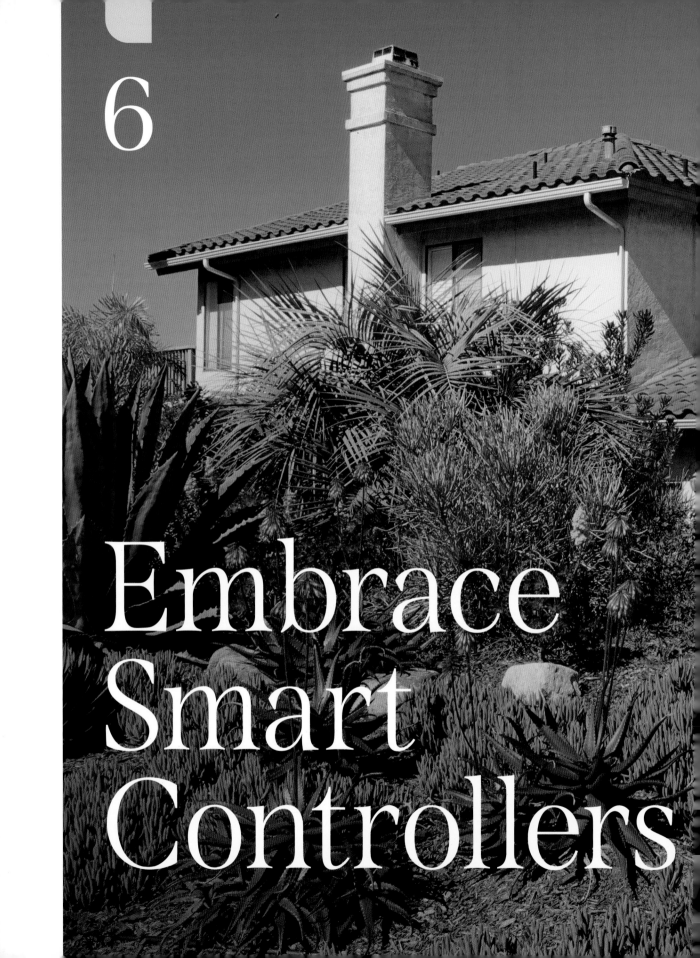

6

Embrace Smart Controllers

EVERY SECOND, THE URBAN POPULATION GROWS by two people. Fifty percent of the world's population lives in cities of 10 million people or more. According to the EPA, landscape irrigation is estimated to account for almost one-third of all residential water use, totaling more than 7 billion gallons per day.

Landscape water use accounts for more than 50 percent of residential water use in the American West and other sunny areas. As a group, we have a giant target on our back. Sooner than later, regulators are going to come for our water. In California, just a 20 percent reduction in landscape water use would be equivalent to lowering all toilet water use to zero. Managing water is an opportunity, but the window of opportunity may close quickly.

We Can Choose Conservation

We all have an opportunity to change the way we manage and use water. However, the chance to make the change is limited. Rising costs and rapidly dwindling natural water supplies are forcing regulators and the government to impose restrictions, taking some options out of our hands. Just drive around any of the neighborhoods in Southern California today and you will see that many people have simply let their landscape go—due to the expensive cost of water. It is accepted by most homeowners that the price of water will only continue to increase.

Take Advantage of Technology

First, we need to embrace technology. Irrigation professionals have seen this crisis coming, and manufacturers of water-monitoring devices have anticipated that average homeowners as well as large-scale agriculture companies will need to take a more active look at water management. Yet only a small percentage of landscape contractors recommend smart controllers to their customers. Less than 15% of the properties I personally visit have a smart controller.

Chapter 5 provides the best argument for installing smart controllers on your property. Yes, in theory, anyone should be able to complete the simple manual calculations needed to determine a reasonable amount of watering time for your home landscape per week. In actuality, it's tedious. The best water managers only do it once every couple of weeks, and even that results in making 26 adjustments a year to a watering system. If you're intimidated by those calculations, consider investing in a smart water controller instead—it'll pay for itself in just a couple of months by the amount it'll save on your water bill.

In most situations, the cheapest and fastest way to save water is by installing and properly using smart controllers. A smart controller measures evapotranspiration data for you and adjusts water distribution daily. You'll see the difference in your water bill—and your garden—in no time. Controllers available on the market range in price and function, just like anything else. Understanding your water management needs will help you select the best controller for your landscape or garden. This chapter provides all the information you need to know to make the best selection.

What Is a Smart Controller?

A smart controller makes daily, real-time adjustments to an irrigation schedule based on evapotranspiration. Evapotranspiration, as defined earlier, is when water is transferred from the soil to the atmosphere—by evaporation from the soil and other surfaces as well as through transpiration from plants. A smart controller can measure the amount of water evaporating daily, and set a watering system to replace the needed amount of water at the appropriate time. The calculation of how much water is lost to evapotranspiration and the proper times to replenish the water varies with the type of controller.

Traditional controllers are typically programmed once a year, and then during specific times of the year (like spring, summer, fall, and winter), they are adjusted down or up accordingly. This allows for only four adjustments a year—compared to a daily or even weekly adjustment. Even if the adjustments were made monthly, this would only require twelve adjustments per year. This chart shows the potential for overwatering and the times of the year it is most prevalent.

The chart above represents proper water use for your landscape. You can see how the applied water equals the monthly ET.

Some smart controllers adjust using one or just a couple of factors. For example, one of those could be a real-time or historical temperature adjustment. For

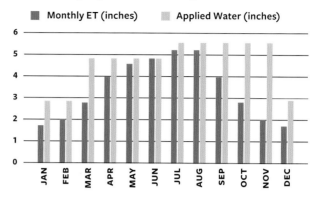

Common industry practice is to program controllers 3–4 times per year and are usually set to overwater

■ Monthly ET (inches) ■ Applied Water (inches)

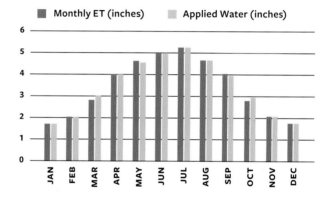

ET-based controllers adjust their own schedule to meet and replenish evapotranspiration losses

■ Monthly ET (inches) ■ Applied Water (inches)

example, if temperatures are rising, the controllers water more. If temperatures are declining, they water less. This makes a difference in your water use but has several setbacks.

If the original program is set for overwatering, your adjustments will save some water, but you will still be overwatering overall. Also, much more goes into evapotranspiration, like wind, humidity, and cloud cover, and using only a few variables will reduce the amount of water you can save. The inaccuracy of this data puts your landscape at risk. This chart provides a visual snapshot only.

What Makes a Smart Controller Smart?

Smart irrigation controllers are based on advanced technology that offers a significant upgrade over traditional or manual irrigation controllers. They are "smart" because of their ability to automatically adjust watering schedules and amounts based on various environmental and soil conditions. Here are the key features that make a smart controller smart:

Weather Data Integration: Smart controllers can adjust irrigation schedules based on real-time weather data. They may use local weather stations, internet-based weather services, or on-site sensors to determine if rain, high winds, or extreme temperatures warrant a change in watering.

Scientifically Generated Irrigation Schedules: Good smart controllers will take the basic information you provide and generate a scientific irrigation schedule from it. This is more beneficial than having the user create and adjust the schedule, which is subject to human error. You will never maximize your water savings if you create a lousy schedule.

Soil Moisture Sensors: Many smart controllers are equipped with—or can be connected to—soil moisture sensors. These sensors provide real-time data on soil moisture levels, allowing the system to water only when necessary, thus preventing overwatering or underwatering.

Evapotranspiration (ET) Tracking: Smart controllers can use historical or real-time ET data to estimate the rate of water loss from soil due to evaporation and plant transpiration, adjusting watering schedules accordingly.

Remote Control and Monitoring: These systems often offer the ability to control and monitor your irrigation system remotely, using a smart phone app or web interface. This feature allows for convenient adjustments and real-time monitoring from anywhere, for everyone.

Customizable Zones: Smart controllers usually include the ability to create multiple watering zones within a landscape, each with a customized watering schedule based on the specific needs of the plants in that zone.

Water Conservation: By optimizing watering schedules and amounts, smart controllers contribute to significant water savings, which is beneficial for the environment and reduces water bills.

Adaptive Learning and Predictive Analytics: Some advanced smart controllers can learn from past data to predict future watering needs. They can adjust their programming based on the learned behaviors of the landscape and weather patterns.

Additionally, smart controllers, depending on manufacturer, can help homeowners benefit in more ways than just water savings. Some smart controllers can:

- *Integrate with Home Automation Systems:* Many smart irrigation controllers can be integrated with broader home automation systems, allowing for centralized control of various home and garden systems.

- *Provide Leak Detection and Alerts:* They can detect leaks or malfunctions in the irrigation system and alert the user, helping to prevent water waste and damage to the landscape.

- *Stay in Compliance with Regulations:* Smart controllers can be programmed to comply with local watering restrictions and drought regulations, automatically adjusting schedules to stay within legal requirements.

The Power of Data

The idea that you can't manage what you can't measure is accurate. Especially when it comes to water. Installing a flow meter will allow a water manager to see how much water is being used in real time. Some smart controllers provide a graphical view of consumption—or fiscal dollars compared with user-defined budgets. When integrated with flow-enabled central controllers, these reports offer daily measured and estimated usage consumption information, so you can see how water usage is stacking up against your budget easily. These also provide the ability to align measured and estimated usage consumption information with the calendar month or the associated water bill service period. This allows users to compare water bill information with measured and estimated usage for tracking and auditing purposes.

A monitoring report is another option that helps take water management to the next level. Users can check the status of a monthly or annual budget at a glance. This interactive interface allows users to review information by account, budget type, actual consumption, unit, month, and year. Water managers can measure and estimate consumption usage aligned with the calendar month or associated water bill service period. Creating reports with the water use graph and the budget monitoring helps water managers keep consistent track of water use. In addition, the ease of exporting the data to a pdf makes it easy to share the information with other water managers and

customers. Providing the data to others is what helps promote meaningful conversations about water. Many discussions concern the value of smart controllers and other water-saving technology available to the landscape industry today. Smart controllers and other water-saving technologies are like an Excel spreadsheet. They are not very valuable by themselves, but when combined with someone who knows how to use the technology, they are extremely valuable.

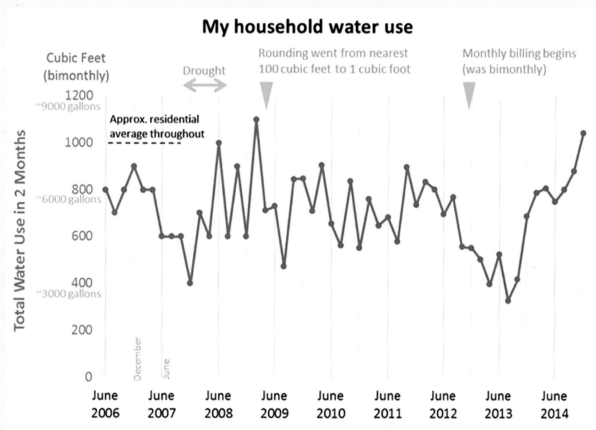

My household water use

My household's total bimonthly water use as shown in our water bills. Although the utility began billing monthly in November 2012, water use is always shown aggregated over two months in this graph throughout the timeline for consistency. My household was on a single 5/8" meter, using drinking water and wastewater service from one utility. Utility raised rates every year and billed for consumption in cubic feet (or 100 cubic feet till April 2009). Meter reading was consistently within 60 days +/- 5 days (94% of the time). The utility's average residential water use during much of this timeline was approximately 1,000 cubic feet bimonthly.

In essence, these controllers' "smart" aspect lies in their ability to use technology and real-time data to make automated, informed decisions about irrigation. This leads to more efficient water use, healthier landscapes, and reduced maintenance effort.

The smartest irrigation controllers also include predictive analytics for potential rainfall. Why water today if it's just going to rain tomorrow? These predictive analytics anticipate rainfall. They calculate how much rainfall is usable and when the rain will occur when scheduling irrigation. It also predicts temperature changes and makes adjustments accordingly. If cooler temperatures are coming, your controller will emit less water than if it looked back at the high ET data from the previous days.

Use a Smart Controller to Manage Water Better

In our quest to address water conservation challenges, it's vital to shift the conversation away from the notion that removing turf or grass and replanting it with clover or native perennials is the sole, best, or easiest solution. Rather, our focus should be on harnessing technology to optimize water usage in order to maintain lush lawns. This approach aligns with the quintessentially American way of tackling challenges—not by banning any one thing, but by innovating and improving.

Consider this analogy with automobiles: We don't advocate banning cars because they consume gasoline. Instead, we set performance goals for fuel efficiency, rewarding companies that provide vehicles that reduce gasoline consumption and benefit the environment. Similarly, we can apply this principle to our lawns, urging homeowners and communities to embrace technology as a means to curtail water consumption while maintaining their green landscapes.

Smart controllers play a pivotal role in this endeavor. These intelligent systems make real-time adjustments based on weather conditions and evapotranspiration data, ensuring that your lawn receives precisely the amount of water it needs. On calm days, the controller tells your system to water less, preventing unnecessary wastage. Unlike conventional controllers, which require manual adjustment roughly four times a year, smart systems automatically suspend watering during rain, freezing temperatures, or high winds. This not only conserves water but also promotes healthier plants with stronger roots, discouraging the growth of weeds, diseases, and fungi.

Furthermore, the benefits of adopting smart controllers extend beyond just water conservation. They save you valuable time by autonomously adjusting watering schedules based on changing weather and soil moisture levels. Additionally, they lead to significant cost savings, potentially reducing your annual

water bill by 30–50%. Many local water utilities even offer rebates if you purchase specific smart controllers, further incentivizing their adoption.

It's time to reframe the discussion—I'm not advocating for the removal of turf, but rather the responsible management of the water used to maintain it. By setting performance standards and embracing technology, we empower homeowners, commercial building owners, and homeowners' associations to be proactive in addressing future water challenges. This approach ensures that our shared goal remains consistent: conserving and saving water. As a side benefit, we get lush, vibrant lawns. Let's transition from a turf removal mentality to water-saving technology, fostering a sense of empowerment and achievement in our communities as we tackle water conservation head-on.

Many people hire landscape contractors to maintain their property. But more contractors are looking into the benefits of smart irrigation systems—it'll benefit their business by taking less staff time to water or maintain a property, and it benefits the environment (by reducing water usage and customer water bills). Some contractors have been apprehensive to install smart controllers in the past, fearing that they might even undercut their business, but that is about to change.

With controller manufacturers continuing to innovate with water management software, it won't be long before every controller will be able to be managed remotely, much like a Nest thermostat. Contractors will realize the benefits of smart irrigation systems, water management, and site management—all can all be achieved much more cheaply, easily, and more accurately with a smart controller.

For years, water management has been thought of as something to handle at an emission-device level, whether that's via pressure-regulated pop-ups, rotors, compensated manifolds, or point source emitters, among others. While these are effective conservation devices, there is an essential next step involved in using these devices properly. The future of the irrigation contractors, like it or not, is heavily influenced by technology and the efficiency of managing multiple sites remotely and accurately.

Some smart controllers can tell us accurately about the amount of water in the soil. As you'll recall from Chapter 4, it's best to irrigate your soil until it reaches "field capacity." Let the water be absorbed into the soil until it hits a

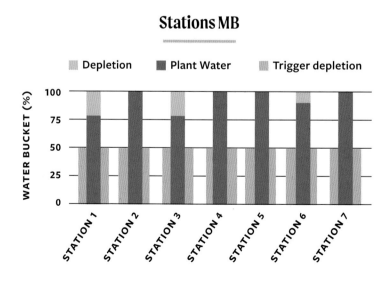

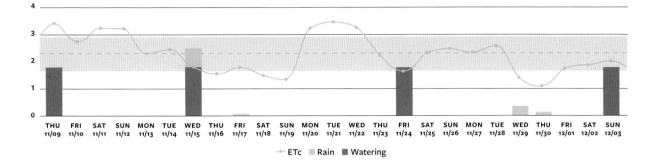

ETc — Rain — Watering

MB for Station 1

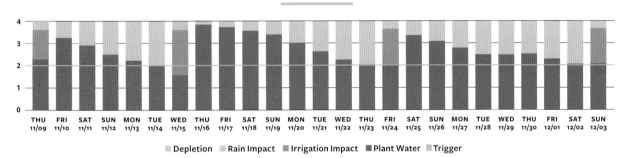

Depletion — Rain Impact — Irrigation Impact — Plant Water — Trigger

maximum allowable depletion, and then fill that soil back up to field capacity. Keep repeating this pattern for the healthiest plants and landscapes.

The graph below shows field capacity as the 100% mark. The maximum allowable depletion is the 50% mark. When the soil moisture reaches 50% of its water-holding potential, the irrigation system is triggered to run. Ensure your plants get water before they reach the permanent wilting point.

Graphs like these grant us humans access to what is happening under the soil line. They also provide a map of when watering needs to happen next. In the graph below, you can see when irrigation occurred and whether water will be following usable rain for your landscape, as well as watch the daily soil water depletion and expected watering days.

Wi-Fi or Cellular Connections

Once you decide to install a smart controller, you'll see that you need to decide between a Wi-Fi smart irrigation controller and a cellular irrigation controller. Which will suit your needs best depends on several factors, including the specific requirements of your irrigation setup, location, and personal preferences. Both have their advantages and potential drawbacks. Here's a comparison to help determine which might be better for your needs:

WI-FI SMART IRRIGATION CONTROLLERS

Advantages:

- *Cost-Effectiveness:* Generally, Wi-Fi controllers are less expensive than cellular controllers.

- *High-Speed Connectivity:* Wi-Fi offers fast data transfer, allowing quicker updates and adjustments.

- *Ease of Integration:* Easily integrates with home Wi-Fi networks and often with other smart home devices and systems.

- *Remote Access:* Offers control and monitoring of your irrigation system via smartphone or computer.

Disadvantages:

- *Dependence on Wi-Fi Range:* Effective only within the range of your Wi-Fi network. Connectivity can be an issue if your garden is far from the router.

- *Susceptibility to Network Issues:* If your home internet goes down, you lose the ability to control the system remotely.

- *Power Dependency:* Generally reliant on a constant power source.

CELLULAR IRRIGATION CONTROLLERS

Advantages:

- *Broader Coverage:* Cellular controllers use mobile networks, so they can be operated in locations far from the house or where Wi-Fi coverage is weak or unavailable.

- *More Reliable Connection:* Less prone to outages than home Wi-Fi systems, making them more reliable for remote locations.

- *Independent Operation:* They can function independently, without relying on a home internet connection.

Disadvantages:

- *Higher Cost:* Cellular controllers typically have a higher up-front cost and may have ongoing expenses tied to cellular service.

- *Data Speed and Limits:* Depending on the cellular plan, data speeds can be slower than Wi-Fi, and data usage limits may exist.

- *Power Requirements:* Like Wi-Fi controllers, they typically need a reliable power source, although some may have battery backup options.

WHICH IS BETTER?

For urban and residential areas: If you are in an urban or residential area with a reliable Wi-Fi network, a Wi-Fi smart irrigation controller might be more suitable for your needs due to its cost-effectiveness and high-speed connectivity.

For remote or large properties: A cellular controller would be preferable, due to its more comprehensive coverage and reliability if the irrigation system is in a remote area or a large property with poor Wi-Fi coverage.

Integration with smart home systems: If you have an existing smart home setup that you want to integrate with your irrigation system, a Wi-Fi controller is likely the better choice.

Conclusion

Ultimately, the "best" option depends on your specific situation. Consider factors like the size and location of your property, the reliability of your internet connection, and whether you need to integrate the controller with other smart home devices. Both Wi-Fi and cellular smart irrigation controllers offer advanced features and convenience, but their effectiveness depends on where and how they will be used.

Smart controllers are revolutionizing the way we manage water, making them an indispensable tool for anyone interested in saving water in their landscapes and gardens. These controllers offer numerous benefits that not only help conserve water but also streamline the irrigation process for more efficient and cost-effective landscaping.

One of the most significant advantages of smart controllers is their ability to manage water effectively. Unlike traditional controllers, smart systems adjust water usage daily based on real-time weather data and evapotranspiration information. This means they provide just the right amount of water based on the actual needs of your landscape, on any given calendar day. Whether it's a calm day or one with adverse weather conditions like rain, freezing temperatures, or high winds, smart controllers automatically suspend watering, thereby preventing

overwatering and conserving water. By minimizing evaporation and encouraging water to soak in, they help reduce the required amount of irrigation, leading to significant water savings.

In addition to water conservation, smart controllers also save you time and money. Once your site data is programmed into the system, the controller will take care of adjusting the watering schedule based on changing weather conditions and soil moisture levels, eliminating the need for constant manual intervention. This not only reduces the hassle of managing your irrigation system but can also lead to substantial cost savings. Smart systems can potentially reduce your annual water bill by 30–50%, making them a wise investment. Many local water providers even offer rebates for purchasing specific smart controllers, further incentivizing their adoption.

Furthermore, smart controllers provide a level of precision and customization that traditional controllers cannot match. They consider various factors including weather data, soil moisture levels, and evapotranspiration rates to create scientifically generated irrigation schedules tailored to your landscape's specific needs. This ensures that your plants receive the right amount of water at the right time, promoting healthier growth and reducing the risk of issues like weeds, diseases, and fungi.

Overall, smart controllers offer an efficient and environmentally responsible way to manage water in your landscapes and gardens. With the potential for substantial water savings, ease of use, and the ability to adapt to changing conditions, these controllers are a valuable addition for those looking to make a quick and cost-effective reduction in water waste. Embracing this technology is a crucial step in addressing water conservation challenges, making it an ideal choice for homeowners, landscape contractors, and anyone committed to a greener future.

7

How to Tell If You Are Overwaterin Underwater Your Plants

OVERWATERING PLANTS is one of the most obvious causes of failure in landscapes today. When plants don't "look healthy," it is tempting to give them more water—but often, this is a mistake. Overwatering mistakes are not easy to diagnose because the symptoms of overwatering, ironically, often mimic the symptoms of a plant that's getting too little water. Overwatering as an ongoing issue also leads to more challenges in your garden and landscape than just water and money waste.

Overwatering can lead to a phenomenon known as "wet soil conditions." It might sound harmless, but these conditions can wreak havoc on your plants. Wet soil conditions occur when the soil is saturated with water for extended periods

of time. While water is of course essential for plant growth, excessively damp soil can harm plants for several reasons.

Soil needs to maintain air pockets. Oxygen hides in these pockets, making itself available to plant roots. When soil is oversaturated with water, water fills the pockets, reducing the oxygen available to the roots. This condition is known as waterlogging. Without oxygen or limited oxygen, your plants will suffer and possibly die.

Prolonged exposure to waterlogged conditions can lead to root rot. The roots of most plants are not designed to live in anaerobic (oxygen-depleted) conditions. Without enough oxygen, roots can die, impairing the plant's ability to absorb nutrients and water. Unless your plant is rice, it's likely not going to be happy to be overwatered.

Overwatering Symptoms

Waterlogged Soil Conditions

Often, we also ignore what overwatering does to fertilizer. Fertilizer is expensive, heavy to transport, and, in many cases, not easy to use. Most of the nitrogen it delivers to soils is simply washed away with excess watering. The goal should be to apply fertilizer and keep it in the root zone for as long as possible. Overwatering leaches essential nutrients from the soil, carrying them away before the plants can utilize them. When water pushes the fertilizer past the root zone, plants take up little of the fertilizer. This nutrient loss can lead to deficiencies, affecting plant health and growth. This deprives our plants of the vital nourishment they need and can also lead to these supercharged nutrients seeping into and contaminating our groundwater. We all know how important it is to feed our plants, but when we over-irrigate, we're potentially increasing our fertilizer costs and wasting our efforts, if these nutrients don't stay where they're needed.

Wet soil creates an ideal environment for the proliferation of certain fungi and pathogens that thrive in moist conditions. This can lead to diseases like root rot and other fungal infections that can harm plant health. In some cases, especially with heavy clay soils, prolonged wetness can lead to soil compaction, where the soil particles are packed too tightly, further reducing aeration and drainage. Clay soil presents some issues for gardeners, and they work hard to reduce the compaction by adding mulch and other organic nutrients to the soil. Don't undo the hard work you put into creating better soil by overwatering.

Our goal is to provide just the right amount of water to plants. I know how I feel when I get hungry. Often, the word "hangry" comes to mind. We are so hungry, we are angry. Our performance is compromised when we are hangry. If we could measure our hunger and provide ourselves just the right amount of snack to head off when we started to get hungry, think of how happy and productive we would be. It's the same for your plants. We want to water them just the right amount (also known as watering them to "field capacity"), monitor the drawdown of water, and give them the right amount just as they get thirsty again. This keeps our plants thriving. Stressed and weakened plants are more susceptible to attacks by pests and diseases, which can further damage or kill the plant. In addition, while we hope for a big harvest of vegetables in the garden, overwatering can reduce productivity. It can hinder your garden's fertility, leaving you with fewer fruits and vegetables to enjoy. And, there is a broader environmental impact. Overwatering can contribute to groundwater contamination, affecting our gardens and the larger ecosystem.

When we overwater our gardens, it doesn't just lead to puddles or mushy soil. It also means we're using more energy, especially if we're using pumping systems, which adds to our energy bills and our environmental footprint.

Ten Signs You're Overwatering

Following are ten easily observable signs that will indicate whether you might be overwatering.

1 Your plant is wilting, but you've been giving it plenty of water.

The roots of plants take up water and oxygen to survive and thrive. Overwatering your plants, in simple terms, drowns your plants. There should be space between the particles of soil in your garden. Normally, oxygen fills this space. Soil that is constantly wet, however, won't have enough air pockets of oxygen, and plants will be unable to breathe by taking up oxygen through their roots. When this occurs, your plants will wilt (giving the appearance of too little water) even though the soil is wet.

The sight of a wilting plant tugs at the heartstrings of any gardener. Surprisingly, both overwatering and underwatering can lead to this seemingly paradoxical phenomenon.

WHY OVERWATERED PLANTS WILT

Contrary to what you might expect, overwatered plants wilt—just like underwatered plants wilt. The reason behind this lies in the plant's physiology:

Root Suffocation: Overwatering leads to waterlogged soil, which hinders the roots' ability to access oxygen. When roots are deprived of oxygen, they cannot function effectively.

Reduced Nutrient Uptake: As root function is impaired, the plant struggles to absorb essential nutrients from the soil. This nutrient deficiency can result in a weakened and wilted appearance.

Leaf Function Is Affected: Wilting occurs because the plant's leaves cannot maintain turgidity—a state of firmness and hydration. Without sufficient water and nutrients, leaves lose their rigidity and droop.

2 The tips of the leaves turn brown.

One of the quickest, first signs that your plants are overwatered is to observe the tip of the leaf turning brown. Overwatering sometimes causes the plant to absorb water faster than it can be used or transpired. This can lead to a buildup of water pressure in the cells at the leaf tips, causing them to burst and turn brown. Root stress is also a possible cause of brown tips. Overwatering often results in waterlogged soil, which can stress the plant's roots. Soggy roots struggle to access oxygen, leading to poor nutrient uptake.

Distinguishing Between Overwatering and Underwatering Wilting:

While wilting can be a shared symptom between over and underwatering, distinguishing between the two is crucial if you want to maintain an overall healthy garden:

Overwatering Wilting:
- Leaves may appear limp and wilted, often with a soft texture.
- Soil is persistently moist and soggy.
- Wilting may be more noticeable on the upper leaves.

Underwatering Wilting:
- Leaves typically become dry and wilted, often with a crispy texture.
- Soil is dry and lacks moisture.
- Wilting may begin at the lower leaves and progress upward.
- Remedy: apply more water.

Addressing Wilting Due to Overwatering:
To address wilting caused by overwatering:

- **Adjust Watering:** Allow the soil to dry out slightly before watering again. Ensure proper drainage to prevent waterlogging.

- **Prune Affected Leaves:** Trim wilted leaves to promote new growth and improve overall plant health.

- **Enhance Soil Aeration:** Improve soil aeration to provide more oxygen to the roots.

- **Fertilize Mindfully:** Consider a balanced fertilizer application to support nutrient uptake.

- **Monitor Recovery:** Observe your plant's progress and adjust your care regimen accordingly.

Wilting due to overwatering may take some time to resolve as the plant recovers from root suffocation and nutrient imbalances. Patience and attentive care will play a vital role in its rejuvenation.

3 Whole leaves turn brown and wilt.

Leaves turn brown and wilt when plants have too little or too much water. The most significant difference is that if plants are receiving too little water, the leaves will feel crispy when you hold them in your hand. Overwatered leaves will feel soft and limp in your hand.

When plants experience leaf browning and wilting due to overwatering or underwatering, several physiological processes are disrupted, leading to these visible symptoms.

In the case of overwatering, the primary issue is that excess water displaces the air in the soil, leading to a lack of oxygen available to the roots. Roots require oxygen to respire and function properly. When they are deprived of oxygen, root respiration is impaired, reducing root function and health. This condition, often leading to root rot, hinders the plant's ability to uptake water and nutrients effectively. Despite the soil being saturated with water, the damaged roots cannot transport sufficient water and nutrients to the leaves, leading to wilting—a phenomenon also known as physiological drought. Furthermore, overwatering creates an environment conducive to fungal and bacterial growth, which can further damage the roots and exacerbate the plant's distress.

Conversely, underwatering leads to a shortage of available moisture in the soil, which means the plant's roots cannot absorb enough water to meet the plant's needs. This lack of water decreases turgor pressure within the plant cells, particularly in the leaves. Turgor pressure is vital for maintaining the structure and firmness of plant cells. When this pressure drops due to insufficient water, the cells lose their rigidity, leading to wilting. Additionally, water is essential for transporting nutrients throughout the plant; thus, underwatering also leads to a nutrient deficiency, contributing to the browning of leaves. The browning typically starts at the tips and edges of the leaves, as these are the farthest parts from the water and nutrient supply routes and are the first to be affected by the deficit.

In both scenarios, the plant's photosynthetic ability can be compromised. Overwatered plants must transport more water and nutrients to the leaves for optimal photosynthesis. In contrast, underwatered plants may close their stomata to conserve water, reducing carbon dioxide intake essential for photosynthesis. If not corrected, both conditions can lead to the deterioration of the plant's health and potentially death. Therefore, maintaining a balanced watering regimen that meets the plant's specific needs is crucial for its health and vitality.

4 Edema

When the roots of plants absorb more water than they can use, water pressure begins to build in the cells of the leaves. The cells will eventually burst, killing them and forming blisters. These areas will look like lesions. Once the blisters

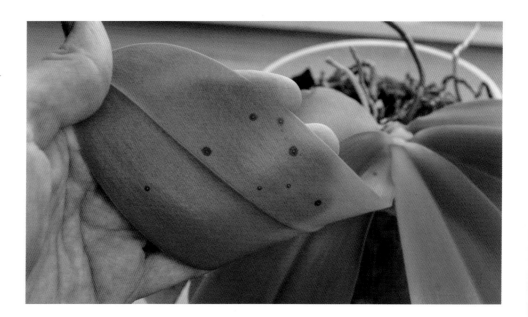

erupt, tan, brown, or white warty growths begin to start where the blisters originally were. Plus, you will see indentations forming directly above the growths on the top sides of the leaves.

Edema, in the context of gardening, is a physiological condition that affects plant cells. It occurs when plant cells absorb more water than they can handle. It's like overeating for plants, but as if they gorge on water instead of food.

Edema is a clear indicator of overwatering because it happens when there's an imbalance between the amount of water available to the plant and its capacity to absorb and process that water. When the soil is consistently saturated due to excessive watering, the plant has more water than it can use.

5 Yellowing leaves

Stunted slow growth with yellowing leaves is a symptom of overwatering your plants. Prevent this by checking up on your plants every few weeks.

Leaves turn yellow when overwatered due to a disruption in the plant's natural processes. Here's how it happens:

Root Suffocation: Overwatering leads to waterlogged soil, which deprives the roots of oxygen. This root suffocation affects the plant's ability to take up essential nutrients like iron.

Iron Deficiency: The roots struggle to absorb iron from the soil without sufficient oxygen. Iron is essential for producing chlorophyll, the green pigment responsible for photosynthesis.

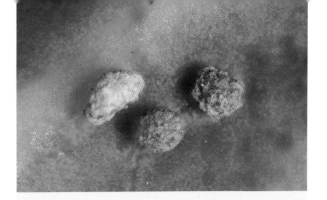

How to Diagnose Edema

Recognizing edema is a valuable skill for any gardener. When a plant experiences edema, you'll notice a few distinct characteristics:

Blisters or Bumps: Edema often manifests as small, raised blisters or bumps on the leaves, stems, or fruit of the plant. These growths may appear as irregular, swollen areas.

Discoloration: The affected areas may also change color. Depending on the plant species, they can turn from green to yellow, brown, or even red.

Detecting edema requires careful observation of your plants. Here's how you can do it:

Inspect the Leaves: Examine the leaves of your plants for any unusual growths, bumps, or discoloration.

Check the Stems: Similarly, inspect the stems of your plants, paying close attention to any irregularities or swollen areas.

Fruit Examination: If you have fruit-bearing plants, check the fruit for any signs of edema, such as raised patches or unusual discoloration.

Chlorophyll Breakdown: As chlorophyll production slows down or halts, the green color fades and leaves turn yellow.

Distinguishing Between Overwatering and Underwatering: Yellowing leaves can also occur due to underwatering, but there are distinct differences to look for:

Overwatering Yellowing:
- Leaves often turn uniformly yellow.
- The yellowing typically starts from the tips or edges and progresses inward.
- The affected leaves may feel soft and appear waterlogged.

Underwatering Yellowing:
- Leaves usually turn yellow in patches or irregular patterns.
- The yellowing often starts from the bottom of the plant and moves upward.
- The affected leaves may become dry and brittle.

What to Do When You Observe Yellowing Leaves: When you notice yellowing leaves, it's essential to take prompt action:

- *Assess Watering:* First, evaluate your watering practices. Determine whether overwatering or underwatering is the likely cause based on the leaf yellowing patterns.

- *Adjust Watering:* If overwatering is the culprit, allow the soil to dry out before watering again. Ensure proper drainage in your pots or garden beds.

- *Provide Nutrients:* Consider applying a balanced, water-soluble fertilizer to replenish essential nutrients for overwatering-induced yellowing.

- *Trim Affected Leaves:* Trim any severely affected leaves to encourage new, healthy growth.

- *Monitor Progress:* Continue to observe your plants and make adjustments as needed. Healthy leaves should gradually regain their green color.

By understanding the reasons behind yellowing leaves and discerning the differences between overwatering and underwatering symptoms, you'll be better equipped to address these issues in your garden. Your attentiveness and timely responses will contribute to your cherished plants' overall health and vitality.

6 Leaf fall

Leaf fall occurs in both situations of too much and too little water. When both young and old leaves fall prematurely, combined with buds not opening, this is a sign of too much water.

Understanding why leaves fall off plants and distinguishing between overwatering and underwatering scenarios is essential.

Physiological Causes of Leaf Loss Due to Overwatering:
Leaves fall off plants when overwatered primarily due to a series of physiological disruptions:

- *Root Suffocation:* Overwatering leads to waterlogged soil, which reduces the oxygen supply to the plant's roots. In response, the roots suffocate, impairing their ability to absorb water and nutrients.

- *Stress Response:* To cope with reduced oxygen levels and nutrient uptake, the plant sheds leaves as a stress response. The plant conserves resources and redirects energy to root recovery by reducing the number of leaves.

Physiological Causes of Leaf Loss Due to Underwatering:

- *Water Stress:* In this case, leaves fall off because the plant is experiencing water stress. When the soil becomes excessively dry, it's challenging for the roots to extract water and maintain turgidity.

- *Energy Conservation:* To conserve water during drought or limited water availability, plants may shed leaves to reduce transpiration (water vapor loss through leaf pores). Fewer leaves mean less water is lost through transpiration.

Differentiating Between Overwatering and Underwatering:
Distinguishing between overwatering and underwatering as the cause of leaf loss can be challenging but crucial:

Overwatering Leaf Loss:
- A yellowing or wilting of leaves may accompany leaf loss.
- Soil may feel excessively wet and poorly drained.
- Overwatered leaves may appear waterlogged, with a soft, mushy texture.

Underwatering Leaf Loss:
- Leaf loss may be accompanied by leaves turning brown and crispy.
- The soil feels dry and crumbly to the touch.
- Stems and remaining leaves may appear wilted but not waterlogged.

Interpreting Leaf Fall:

All plants sometimes lose leaves as a natural part of their growth and development. To determine if the leaf fall is excessive, consider the following factors:

- *Seasonal Variations:* Some plants shed leaves seasonally, such as deciduous trees in the fall. This is normal and should not cause concern.

- *Consistency:* If leaf loss occurs consistently throughout the year, it may indicate a problem with watering or another environmental factor.

- *Leaf Density:* Evaluate the overall density of leaves on the plant. A gradual decrease in leaf density may be a natural response to changing seasons.

- *New Growth:* Monitor the appearance of fresh leaves. If the plant continually produces healthy new growth, it's likely to effectively cope with leaf loss.

What to Do About Leaf Loss:

- *Adjust Watering:* Determine whether overwatering or underwatering is the issue and adjust your watering regimen accordingly.

- *Fertilize:* Consider providing balanced fertilizer to support root and leaf recovery.

- *Prune Dead Material:* Trim away dead or fallen leaves to prevent disease and improve air circulation.

- *Monitor Continuously:* Keep a close eye on your plants and make necessary adjustments as they recover.

By understanding the physiological processes behind leaf loss and observing your plants, you'll be better equipped to respond to their needs and promote their overall well-being. Remember that some leaf loss is a natural part of a plant's life cycle, but consistent or excessive leaf loss may indicate underlying issues that require your attention.

7   Moldy Soil

Organic material benefits soil health by contributing to nutrient content, improving soil structure, and enhancing moisture retention. However, not all forms of organic matter have positive effects. Mold in soil, particularly in excess, can be problematic for several reasons.

Plant Diseases: Some molds are pathogenic and can cause diseases in plants. These molds can infect plant roots, leaves, and stems, leading to root rot, damping-off in seedlings, or foliage diseases. While a healthy soil ecosystem includes a balance of microorganisms, including some mold, an overabundance of pathogenic molds can harm plant health.

Imbalance of Soil Microflora: Soil is a complex ecosystem containing a diverse range of microorganisms, including bacteria, fungi (like mold), protozoa, and others. These organisms play various roles in nutrient cycling, decomposition, and soil structure maintenance. An overgrowth of mold can disrupt this balance, potentially outcompeting beneficial microorganisms and altering the soil's microbial community in ways that are not conducive to plant health.

Toxin Production: Some molds produce mycotoxins, which are toxic compounds that can harm plants, humans, and animals. These toxins can inhibit seed germination, reduce plant growth, and cause other physiological problems.

Reduced Oxygen Levels: Mold growth on the soil surface can create a dense mat that inhibits gas exchange. This can reduce the oxygen levels in the soil, which is essential for root respiration and the activity of beneficial aerobic soil organisms.

Nutrient Competition: Molds, like other living organisms, require nutrients to grow. When mold growth is excessive, molds can compete with plants for essential nutrients, potentially leading to nutrient deficiencies for the plants.

It's important to distinguish between the natural and beneficial decomposition of organic matter by a balanced soil microbial community and the overgrowth of certain molds that can be harmful. Good soil management practices, such as ensuring proper drainage, avoiding overwatering, and maintaining healthy soil pH and nutrient levels, can help prevent dangerous mold growth while promoting the beneficial decomposition of organic matter.

Mold in soil can be a sign of overwatering, but it can also result from other factors.

Causes of Mold in Soil:

Mold in soil is primarily caused by excessive moisture and organic matter. Here's how it happens:

- *Excessive Moisture:* Overwatering leads to waterlogged soil, creating a consistently damp environment that promotes mold growth.

- *Organic Matter:* Mold feeds on organic matter in the soil, such as decaying plant material or organic mulch. When moisture levels are high, mold thrives and multiplies.

- *Poor Drainage:* Inadequate drainage can exacerbate mold growth by trapping water in the soil.

Distinguishing Mold from Other Soil Issues:

Mold in soil can resemble other soil issues, such as algae, slime molds, or fungal diseases. Here's how to distinguish mold from these problems:

- *Mold Appearance:* Mold typically appears as fuzzy or powdery growth on the soil's surface and is often white, gray, or greenish. It may also produce a musty odor.

- *Algae and Slime Molds:* Algae can create green, slimy patches on the soil's surface. Slime molds appear as gelatinous, colorful masses. Both thrive in damp conditions.

- *Fungal Diseases:* Plant fungal diseases often affect plants, causing symptoms such as yellowing leaves or wilting. Soil mold is distinct from plant diseases.

Addressing Mold in Soil:

To address mold in soil and prevent its recurrence:

- *Moderate Watering:* Adjust your watering routine to avoid overwatering. Allow the soil to dry out slightly between watering sessions.

- *Improve Drainage:* Ensure proper drainage by using well-draining soil mixes, pots with drainage holes, and elevating containers slightly off the ground.

- *Aerate the Soil:* Gently cultivate the soil's surface to improve aeration and reduce moisture retention.

- *Mulch Mindfully:* Avoid overapplication when using mulch, as excess mulch can trap moisture. Use mulch that allows for air circulation.

- *Prune Affected Areas:* Remove moldy soil or affected plant debris from the surface and dispose of it properly. Replace with fresh, healthy soil if necessary.

- *Sterilize Containers:* If mold persists in pots or containers, sterilize them with a dilute bleach solution, allowing them to dry thoroughly and use fresh soil.

- *Increase Air Circulation:* Ensure adequate air circulation around potted plants, especially indoor plants.

8 Mushy Stems

Mushy stems in plants can be a sign of overwatering but can also result from other factors. In this section, we'll explore why stems become mushy due to overwatering, how to differentiate them from other issues, and what actions to take when confronted with mushy stems.

Causes of Mushy Stems Due to Overwatering:

Mushy stems in plants typically occur when overwatering leads to root suffocation and stem rot. Here's how it happens:

- *Root Suffocation:* Overwatering causes waterlogged soil, depriving plant roots of essential oxygen. Roots need oxygen to function correctly.

- *Impaired Nutrient Uptake:* In saturated conditions, roots cannot effectively absorb nutrients, leading to a nutrient imbalance within the plant.

- *Fungal and Bacterial Growth:* Excess moisture creates a conducive environment for fungal and bacterial pathogens to thrive. These pathogens can infect the plant's stem, causing it to become spongy and rot.

- *Collapsing Cell Structure:* Over time, excess moisture can cause plant cells in the stem to break down, leading to a mushy texture.

Distinguishing Mushy Stems from Other Issues:

Mushy stems should be differentiated from other stem-related problems, such as mechanical damage, disease, or pest infestations. Here's how to distinguish mushy stems due to overwatering:

- *Mushy Stem Appearance:* Mushy stems will feel soft and may appear discolored. The mushiness is typically uniform along the stem.

- *Mechanical Damage:* Mechanical damage often results in visible cuts, tears, or breaks on the stem.

- *Disease or Pest Damage:* Disease or pest damage may result in irregular damage patterns on the stem, such as lesions, spots, or chewed areas.

Addressing Mushy Stems:

To address mushy stems caused by overwatering and prevent further damage:

- *Assess Watering Practices:* Adjust your watering routine to allow the soil to dry out between watering sessions. Ensure proper drainage in pots and garden beds.

- *Prune Affected Areas:* Carefully remove the mushy portions of any stems using sterilized pruning shears. Make clean cuts to prevent further infection.

- *Treat with Fungicides:* If fungal or bacterial pathogens are suspected, consider treating the plant with appropriate fungicides or bactericides following label instructions.

- *Improve Air Circulation:* Ensure proper air circulation around the plant to reduce moisture and prevent future fungal growth.

- *Monitor Recovery:* Keep a close eye on the plant as it recovers. Adjust watering practices and provide appropriate care to support its rehabilitation.

9 Fungus Gnats

Fungus gnats are tiny flying insects that are often associated with overwatered soil. Fungus gnats (*Bradysia spp.*) are small, dark-colored flies, typically measuring about ⅛ inch in length. They are often found around houseplants, outdoor gardens, and greenhouses.

Why Fungus Gnats Indicate Overwatering:

Fungus gnats are closely linked to overwatered soil because their larvae thrive in moist environments. Here's how their presence can be a sign of overwatering:

- *Moisture Requirement:* Fungus gnat larvae (the immature stage) require consistently damp soil to survive and develop. Overwatered soil provides the ideal environment for their growth.

- *Organic Matter:* The larvae feed on organic matter within the soil, such as decaying plant material and fungi. Overwatering can promote the decomposition of organic matter, attracting these pests.

What Fungus Gnats Do to Your Plants:

While adult fungus gnats primarily feed on decaying organic matter, their larvae can harm your plants in several ways:

- *Root Damage:* Fungus gnat larvae feed on plant roots and root hairs. This can weaken the plant and hinder its ability to absorb water and nutrients.

- *Disease Transmission:* Fungus gnats can carry and transmit diseases, such as root rot and fungal pathogens, from one plant to another.

Where Do Fungus Gnats Come From?

- *Infested Soil:* They may already bes present in the soil or potting mix you use for your plants.

- *Outdoor Entry:* Fungus gnats can enter your indoor space through open windows and doors if they are prevalent in the surrounding environment.

How to Get Rid of Fungus Gnats:
Effective control of fungus gnats involves several strategies:

- *Reduce Overwatering:* Adjust your watering practices to ensure the soil surface dries out between watering. This deprives the larvae of their preferred moist environment.

- *Allow for Drainage:* Use well-draining potting mixes and containers with drainage holes to prevent waterlogged soil.

- *Monitor Soil:* Keep a close eye on the top layer of soil for any signs of adult gnats or their larvae.

- *Use Yellow Sticky Traps:* Place yellow sticky traps near your plants to capture adult gnats.

- *Biological Control:* Introduce beneficial nematodes or predatory insects (such as rove beetles) that feed on fungus gnat larvae.

- *Neem Oil:* Apply neem oil to the soil surface to deter adult gnats from laying eggs.

- *Diatomaceous Earth:* Sprinkle food-grade diatomaceous earth on the soil surface to deter adult gnats.

- *Avoid Overcrowding:* Space your plants appropriately to promote air circulation and reduce humidity.

10 Slow Growth

Detecting slow growth in a plant can be done by observing several key indicators:

Size: Compare the plant's current size to what would be expected for its age or species. Slow-growing plants will be noticeably smaller than their counterparts of the same age.

Leaf Size: Check the size of the leaves. Slow-growing plants often have smaller leaves than healthy, fast-growing ones.

Internode Length: Measure the distance between leaves or branches along the stem. Short internodes indicate slow growth.

Color: Examine the color of the leaves. Slow-growing plants may have faded or pale green leaves compared to vibrant, healthy plants.

Sparse Foliage: If the plant has fewer leaves and branches than expected, it's likely experiencing slow growth.

Water-wise, Slow Growth Can Be Caused by Several Factors Related to Watering:

- *Overwatering:* One of the leading causes of slow growth is overwatering. Soil that is consistently waterlogged can suffocate the roots and hinder their ability to take up essential nutrients.

- *Underwatering:* Conversely, underwatering can also slow growth. Insufficient moisture can stress the plant and limit its ability to carry out essential processes like photosynthesis.

- *Poor Drainage:* Plants in pots or containers with inadequate drainage can suffer from slow growth due to water accumulating at the root zone.

- *Inappropriate Watering Schedule:* Providing water on a consistent schedule or adjusting the watering frequency based on the plant's needs can also result in slow growth.

To Address Slow Growth in Your Plants:

- *Review Watering Practices:* Ensure you water your plants appropriately for their species and environmental conditions. Allow the soil to dry out slightly between waterings to prevent overwatering.

- *Check Soil Quality:* Assess the soil quality to ensure it is well-draining and provides adequate aeration to the roots.

- *Fertilize Mindfully:* Use a balanced, water-soluble fertilizer to provide essential nutrients that may be lacking in the soil. Follow the recommended application rates and frequency.

- *Prune and Trim:* Regularly prune dead or unhealthy growth to encourage new growth and allocate the plant's energy more effectively.

- *Monitor Light Levels:* Ensure your plants receive the appropriate light for their species. Inadequate light can also lead to slow growth.

You can encourage healthier and more vigorous growth by carefully observing your plant's growth patterns, addressing watering-related issues, and providing optimal growing conditions.

Underwatering Symptoms

Unfortunately, the signals you receive from your plants for underwatering are similar to those when you overwater plants. Often, underwatering and overwatering plants present the same symptoms: sick or dead leaves. Below are some critical signs that will help you determine if you are overwatering or underwatering your plants.

The Soil Is Dry

A simple solution for testing soil moisture is a long screwdriver. Walk your property and press a screwdriver into the ground. When the soil is moist, the screwdriver should penetrate the soil easily. The penetration depth will vary by the soil type, the screwdriver size, and your strength. But as any the soil dries up, the screwdriver will be harder and harder to push into the soil.

Footprints Remain Visible on Turf

Walk across your lawn late in the day, then turn around and examine the lawn behind you. If your steps left any "footprints," that means the grass blades have low water levels in their tissues. When the grass blades are compressed by your feet, the low water levels prevent the grass blades from springing back up. If your footprints remain on the lawn for an extended period, the lawn should be watered to prevent the grass from becoming dormant or possibly dying.

However, it's important to note that similar symptoms can be caused by other factors such as underwatering, pest infestations, nutrient deficiencies, or environmental stressors. To accurately diagnose the problem, consider the following:

Soil Moisture: Check if the soil is consistently wet. Overwatered soil will often feel soggy and may have a musty smell, indicating root rot.

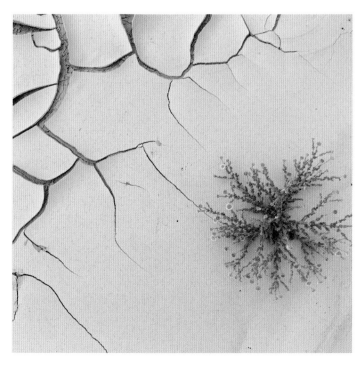

Root Inspection: Gently remove the plant from its pot and inspect the roots. Healthy roots are typically white and firm. Brown, mushy, or odorous roots suggest overwatering and root rot.

Watering Schedule: Reflect on your watering habits. Overwatering is more likely if you water on a schedule without checking soil moisture levels or if the soil lacks proper drainage.

Environmental Conditions: Low light and cool temperatures reduce the plant's water needs. Overwatering is more likely under these conditions if watering is not adjusted accordingly.

Correct diagnosis is critical to addressing the issue effectively. If overwatering is the problem, reduce your watering frequency, ensure good drainage, and allow the soil to dry out somewhat between watering.

How Do You Fix Watering Issues?

Check your soil regularly. Don't be afraid to push your finger into the soil and see how moist it is an inch or two down. If the soil is wet and you have some of the conditions above, it's a sign to reduce your water. Also, many stores sell inexpensive but accurate moisture meters. Insert them in the root ball of any pant, and they will tell you how much water is in the soil. This simple tool will take much of the guesswork out of watering your landscape. The key to soil moisture meters is ensuring you get to where the roots live. For example, if you have tomatoes that have a root depth of 18 inches, you need a soil moisture meter that is at least 18 inches long.

Knowing ETo and ETc values helps with overwatering tremendously, as discussed in earlier chapters. Now you know how much water your plants need, scientifically speaking, and can quickly determine if you are watering too much or too little. As a result, when you see signs of overwatering or underwatering, intuitively, you will be able to identify the root problem. If you have been watering daily and ET is low, it will likely mean that you're overwatering. If you haven't watered for a while and your plant shows signs like brown tips or wilting, it's going to be an underwatering issue.

By understanding the impacts of under and overwatering on plants, we know the plant-water relationship better. Overwatering suffocates plant roots by displacing soil air, reducing oxygen availability, root rot, and subsequent wilting and leaf browning. This excess moisture also fosters fungal and bacterial growth, harming the roots. Conversely, underwatering results in inadequate soil moisture, causing a decline in turgor pressure and wilting within plant cells. The limited water availability also hampers nutrient transport, contributing to leaf browning. Both conditions disrupt photosynthesis and overall plant health. Understanding the delicate balance of soil moisture is crucial, as it influences root health, nutrient uptake, and the plant's ability to thrive. Proper watering practices tailored to the specific needs of each plant will maintain optimal soil conditions and ensure plant health.

8

How to Tell If You Are Overfertiliz Your Plants

TO HELP UNDERSTAND WHY FERTILIZATION is included in a book about water management, it is critical to be able to identify the signs of overfertilization, which can mimic signs of overwatering. When too much fertilizer is applied, plants have more difficulty absorbing water. In addition, overfertilized plants often require more water to cope with nutrient imbalances impacting water conservation efforts. We water in fertilizer and drip fertilizer into our landscapes and gardens using fertigation.

Water pollution is another issue we are concerned about. Nitrogen use efficiency (NUE) measures how effectively a plant utilizes available nitrogen from the soil for growth and development. It assesses the ratio of the amount of nitrogen in the harvested parts of the plant to the total amount of nitrogen available to the plant, either from the soil or added fertilizers. High NUE indicates efficient nitrogen use, leading to better crop yields and reduced environmental impact due to lesser nitrogen waste and runoff. Across the country, around 45 percent of fertilizer is washed into the water table, clearly a big concern. I have seen firsthand, after testing water pumped for agriculture, situations where no nitrogen application is needed due to the amount of nitrogen already in the water. Some farmers do not have to apply nitrogen because there is enough nitrogen in the water irrigating their plants. However, the high nitrogen content in the water is due to poor water use efficiency.

Proper fertilization of gardens and landscapes is essential for several reasons. First, it ensures plants receive the necessary nutrients for healthy growth and development. Fertilizers provide crucial elements like nitrogen, phosphorus, and potassium (vital for various plant functions), including root development, flower, fruit production, and overall plant vigor. Balanced fertilization leads to healthier plants, more vibrant flowers, and bountiful harvests in vegetable gardens.

Second, responsible fertilizer use is crucial for environmental sustainability. Overfertilization can lead to nutrient runoff into waterways, causing eutrophication and harming aquatic ecosystems. By applying fertilizers correctly, gardeners and landscapers can minimize environmental impact, reducing the risk of water pollution and preserving natural resources. Using fertilizers judiciously also helps maintain soil health by preventing nutrient imbalances and salt buildup, which can degrade soil quality over time.

Third, efficient fertilization practices contribute to water conservation. There is a proper amount of growth that is normal for plants. Attempting to force plants to grow either too fast or too large wastes water and labor. You will just have to prune those plants back more often. Plants that receive the right nutrients are better equipped to utilize water efficiently. Overfertilized plants often require more water to compensate for excess nutrients, leading to wasteful water usage. In contrast, adequately fertilized plants can make the most of available water, reducing the need for frequent watering and helping conserve this precious resource. Therefore, understanding and implementing appropriate fertilization techniques benefits the plants and supports more comprehensive efforts in water conservation and environmental stewardship.

Understanding Fertilizers

Below is a list of the most common types of fertilizers used in our home gardens and landscapes. Fertilizers are crucial to maintaining healthy plants and provide essential nutrients that plants need to grow. There are various types of fertilizers available, and each has a different benefit. Here are some common types:

Granular Fertilizers: These are dry pellets that release nutrients slowly over time. They are applied to the soil and can provide nourishment over several months. Granular fertilizers can be either fast-release, which provides nutrients quickly but requires more frequent application, or slow-release, which provides a steady supply of nutrients over a more extended period.

Liquid Fertilizers: These are concentrated liquids mixed with water and applied to the plants' soil or foliage. Liquid fertilizers are absorbed quickly, making them ideal for giving plants a quick boost or addressing nutrient deficiencies.

Organic Fertilizers: Derived from natural sources such as compost, manure, bone meal, or cottonseed meal, organic fertilizers improve soil structure and increase water retention capacity. They release nutrients slowly and improve the biodiversity of the soil by encouraging beneficial microbial activity.

Synthetic/Inorganic Fertilizers: These artificial fertilizers can provide nutrients to plants quickly. They are often high in nutrients like nitrogen, phosphorus, and potassium, which are essential for plant growth. However, they do not improve long-term soil health and can lead to salt buildup if used excessively.

Balanced Fertilizers: These contain equal amounts of the primary nutrients: nitrogen (N), phosphorus (P), and potassium (K). The N-P-K ratio on the packaging might look like 10-10-10 or 20-20-20. Balanced fertilizers are versatile and can be used for various plants.

Specialized Fertilizers: Some fertilizers are formulated for specific plants or growth stages, such as starter fertilizers for seeding or transplanting or bloom boosters with higher phosphorus content for flowering plants.

Time-Release Fertilizers: Also known as controlled-release fertilizers, these are coated granules that dissolve over time and release nutrients gradually. They reduce the risk of over-fertilization and minimize the frequency of application.

Foliar Fertilizers: Applied directly to plant leaves, foliar fertilizers can be absorbed quickly through the foliage. They help correct mid-season nutrient deficiencies.

Water-Soluble Fertilizers: These dissolve in water and are used for a quick, uniform distribution of nutrients. They can be applied with a watering can, a hose-end sprayer, or irrigation system.

Soil Amendments: While not fertilizers in the traditional sense, soil amendments like lime, gypsum, and sulfur can alter soil pH and improve its nutrient availability, indirectly influencing plant nutrition.

Each type of fertilizer has its appropriate application and ideal conditions for use. Gardeners should choose based on their plants' needs, soil conditions, and environmental impact preferences. I always recommended performing a soil test before applying any fertilizer to understand what nutrients are needed. Review soil testing in Chapter 2 if you need a refresher on how to help determine what kind of soil you have.

Plants primarily absorb nutrients from fertilizers through a process known as root absorption. For this to occur effectively, the nutrients must first be solubilized in water, as roots uptake nutrients in a liquid form. This is why we water in fertilizer after application. The solubility of fertilizer components is critical in their availability to plants. Once dissolved, the nutrients are transported across the root cell membranes through passive and active transport mechanisms. Soil moisture acts as a conduit for these nutrients, highlighting why consistent watering is essential after applying fertilizer. Without adequate moisture, the nutrients remain locked in the soil's solid components, unavailable to the plant.

Fertilizers serve a dual purpose; not only do they provide essential nutrients directly to plants, but they also enhance the fertility of the soil itself. Over time, as plants grow and produce, they deplete the soil of its nutrient reserves. Fertilizers replenish these stores, ensuring the soil remains a robust medium for plant growth. The continuous cycle of growth, harvest, and soil rejuvenation with fertilizers supports sustainable plant production. Moreover, fertilizers can help repair soils compromised by erosion or leaching, often washing away charged particles that hold nutrients. By restoring the nutrient density of the soil, fertilizers enable it to support healthy and vigorous plant growth, which is crucial for both natural ecosystems, productivity, and aesthetics.

Do Fertilizers Contain Salt?

A lot of people believe salts kill plants, and worry that there are salts in fertilizers.

Yes, many fertilizers contain salts, but fertilizer salts are not the same as table salt. In the context of chemistry and soil science, "salt" refers to any chemical compound composed of cations (positively charged ions) and anions (negatively charged ions) that dissociate in water. Fertilizers commonly contain salts of essential nutrients such as nitrogen, phosphorus, and potassium, all of which are vital to plant growth.

For instance, a standard nitrogen fertilizer, ammonium nitrate, has the chemical formula NH_4NO_3 and dissociates into ammonium (NH_4^+) and nitrate (NO_3^-) ions when dissolved in water. Similarly, potassium chloride, a common source of potassium for plants, is a salt that dissociates into potassium (K^+) and chloride (Cl^-) ions.

While salts are necessary for providing plants with essential nutrients, excessive amounts can be harmful. High concentrations of salts can lead to a condition known as "fertilizer burn," essentially a dehydration effect caused by the salts drawing water away from plant roots and tissues. Salinity can also affect soil structure, reducing its ability to hold water and nutrients, and may impact the soil's microbiome.

To minimize potential salt damage, following recommended fertilizer application rates and schedules and ensuring adequate irrigation to help dissolve and distribute the salts properly is essential. Additionally, using organic fertilizers can help mitigate the impact of salt on plants and soil because these natural options often have lower salt indexes than synthetic fertilizers.

Signs of Overfertilization

Too much water, too little water, and too much fertilizer look similar. Take a look at the leaves on the tomato plant curling in the image opposite. It could be from one of three factors. However, as the water manager and caretaker for the plants,

you know the history of what kind of watering has occurred. You also know your soil, because you've done a test to review and determine whether too much nitrogen has been applied.

This turf is experiencing burn due to too much nitrogen. This condition may develop after a heavy fertilization. Again, at first glance you might assume the turf is suffering from too little water, but thoroughly understanding how the landscape has been managed will simplify troubleshooting the issue.

Distinguishing between signs of underwatering and overfertilization can be challenging as they share similar symptoms like wilting, leaf browning, and stunted growth. However, there are ways to differentiate:

Soil Examination: Check the soil moisture. If the soil is dry and crumbly, underwatering is likely. Conversely, if you see a white, crusty layer of fertilizer salts on the soil surface, it points to over-fertilization.

Fertilization History: Consider your recent fertilization practices. Overfertilization is probable if you've applied fertilizer more frequently or in larger quantities than recommended.

Root Inspection: Carefully examine the roots. If they are brittle or brown, it could be due to overfertilization. Healthy roots in need of water are usually pliable but dry.

Leaf Symptoms: Both conditions can cause leaf browning, but the pattern may differ. Overfertilization often leads to leaf tip and edge burn, whereas underwatering might cause uniformly dry, crispy leaves.

Plant Recovery Response: Monitor how the plant responds to watering. If symptoms improve after watering, it is likely underwatered. Over-fertilization might be the issue if there's no change or a worsening condition.

Water Runoff: Overfertilized soil may repel water, causing it to run off rather than absorb. This doesn't happen with just underwatered soil.

Always cross-check these signs to diagnose the problem accurately.

Osmotic Stress and Plant Health

Plants cannot take up water if there's too much fertilizer in the soil. Plants rely on an osmotic pressure gradient to collect water. That is, when the concentration of dissolved solids rises continuously from the soil around the roots to the core of the root, this causes water to flow into the plant. The water flow reverses when the pressure around the roots gets too high. This is where the term "burning your plants" comes from. The water flows from the leaves out through the roots, and the leaves burn because they don't have water to cool them.

Plants adjust to variations in the level of nutrients around their roots, but they do best when the level is consistent. This is one of the main benefits of fertigation. Fertigation provides a little fertilizer each time you water so the level around the root stays consistent. This is much better than occasionally shocking your plants with fertilizer. Plants are just like us. We perform better and feel better when we don't get too full or hungry. Moderation is the key for our plants and ourselves.

Too much fertilizer can be bad for the environment. Excess fertilizers are leached into our groundwater, rivers, and oceans if you add too many nutrients. This is a concern for people with few plants because, cumulatively, the amount adds up quickly in landscapes. Farmers are concerned, too, because many use large amounts of nitrogen for their crops.

Corrective Measures

To leach excess salts from the soil, there's a best practice called "leaching irrigation." This involves applying water in sufficient quantity that it will penetrate beyond the root zone, carrying excess salts with it. Here's how to effectively implement leaching irrigation:

Deep, Infrequent Watering: Apply water deeply and less frequently. This encourages the water to percolate through the soil, dissolving and carrying salts past the root zone. The amount of water required depends on the soil type, salinity level, and the crop's tolerance to salt.

Even Distribution: Water should be distributed evenly across a given planting bed or area to prevent uneven salt distribution. Drip irrigation or soaker hoses can be effective, but overhead irrigation might be more uniform for leaching.

Monitor Soil Moisture: Avoid waterlogging the soil. Use soil moisture sensors or manual methods to ensure the soil is moist but not saturated. Overwatering can cause other issues, like root rot.

Post-Leaching Care: Give the soil time to drain before regular watering resumes. Also, monitor the plants for any stress signs and adjust the irrigation practices accordingly.

Regular Monitoring: Periodically test the soil for salinity to determine if additional leaching is needed and to adjust your everyday irrigation practices to prevent salt buildup.

Leaching should be done carefully, taking local water conservation regulations and environmental impacts into consideration. It's a balancing act between removing excess salts and maintaining sustainable water use practices.

How to Save an Overfertilized Plant

When you get carried away with fertilizer or discover that you have a buildup of fertilizer in your potted plants, there are some steps you can take to save them. First, leach the fertilizer out of the soil with a long watering, taking the fertilizer out of the root zone or out the bottom of the pot. If there is a crust of fertilizer on the soil's surface, remove it carefully—manually. But don't take off more than ¼ of the topsoil with it. Remove any wilted and burned leaves. Stop fertilizing and rethink the amount you are using. You have a good chance of saving the plant!

Long, deep watering helps leach salts out of the soil by moving water through the soil profile. As water percolates down, it dissolves the salts and carries them deeper into the soil and eventually beyond the root zone. This process gradually reduces the concentration of salts around plant roots, alleviating the potential for salt-induced stress and damage to plants. Regular deep watering, especially in soils with good drainage, effectively manages salt accumulation in the root zone.

Preventive Strategies

As you can tell, a soil test is crucial to success in gardening, your landscape, or your farm. Be sure to test your soil before the season starts. If your soil contains too much nitrogen or too much of any of the other essential elements for growth, you will know before preparing the soil. There are sixteen essential plant nutrients, vital for plant growth and development, each playing a unique role in various physiological processes. They are typically categorized into macronutrients, which are needed in more significant amounts (such as nitrogen, phosphorus, potassium, calcium, magnesium, and sulfur), and micronutrients, required in smaller quantities (such as iron, manganese, zinc, copper, molybdenum, boron, chlorine, and nickel). Proper balance and availability of these nutrients are crucial for healthy plant growth. Too little or too much will impact plant growth.

Understanding Fertilizer Labels and Application Rates

For indoor growers, people growing vegetable gardens or fruit trees, general ornamental gardeners, and landscapers alike, fertilizer is a critical success factor. There is an overwhelming variety amount of fertilizers to choose from today, but learning some basic concepts about fertilizer will make your edible garden produce more food and your landscape more beautiful. Below is a great start to help you dive into a subject that significantly impacts food production and water use.

4-6-3: What Do These Numbers Mean?

These numbers correspond to the percentage of nitrogen, phosphorus, and potassium in the product you are buying. This is often referred to as NPK. An easy way to remember the order of what each letter (NPK) represents is that they are in alphabetical order: nitrogen, phosphorus, and potassium. NPK refers to their atomic symbols on the periodic table of elements.

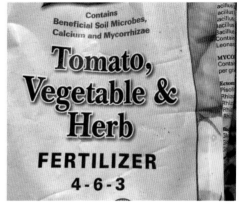

So, if the numbers on the fertilizer container are 4-6-3, that means 4% of the contents of the container by weight are nitrogen, 6% are phosphorus, and 3% are potassium. Each element impacts your garden differently, and understanding the amounts and differences is critical to gardening success. These numbers don't add up to 100% (we see you, math majors), because there are other nutrients and fillers in the container.

Say your garden needs five pounds of nitrogen (thanks to a soil test, you know this). If you have 4-6-3 fertilizer, that means you would need five bags. Each 25-pound bag contains 4% nitrogen, which equates to 1 pound of nitrogen per bag. Therefore, to achieve the desired 5 pounds of nitrogen, you would use five bags of this fertilizer.

Nitrogen

Nitrogen helps plants grow healthy green foliage and stems. The amount of nitrogen needed varies by plant. Too much nitrogen may give lush green leaves but inhibit blooms or fruit. There are many variables in this formula, and it takes some experimenting to get it "right," but an excellent way to speed up the process is to test your soil.

Phosphorus

Phosphorus increases your plant's ability to flower and the bloom size and promotes strong, healthy roots. Newly transplanted plants and young plantings often benefit from phosphorus fertilizer. The highest phosphorus fertilizer you can use is 61%. But remember that too much of anything can be a bad thing. Too much phosphorus can stimulate algae growth and make it hard for plants to take up other essential nutrients, like iron and zinc. Try to resist the temptation to blast your plants with more of everything—with fertilizer, more is not more.

Potassium

Potassium is also essential for your plants. It helps fight off diseases and helps with water management by providing drought protection. A great time to use potassium is after your plants are damaged by disease or insects.

One problem with fertilizers is that many people overdo it, thinking if some fertilizer is good, more must be better. Another misconception is that fertilizer will heal a sick plant. So you dump fertilizer on, but then the plant suffers from overwatering, a virus, or bad soil pH. A good soil test will help you understand your exact problem so you can tailor your application of fertilizer appropriately rather than blanket an area with something your plants may not need—or want.

Finally, if your soil is rich in organic matter, beneficial bacteria, and fungi because you've been applying compost regularly, you will have to fertilize less often or not at all. Compost and what constitutes healthy, living soil is the subject of a longer conversation than we can tackle here; do some simple online research to ensure you give your plants vital amounts of organic compounds.

Fertilizer and water management are directly and closely related. A good understanding of both principles ensures success in your garden and landscape. The best way to determine issues in your garden related to water and fertilizer is to review your past processes and have a soil test performed. This will help identify the issue and allow you to take proper steps to reduce or eliminate the problems.

9

Simple Adjustments Your Irrigation System That Will Save Water and Money

BY PERFORMING JUST A FEW SIMPLE ADJUSTMENTS to your sprinkler system, you will save gallons upon gallons of water. And a bonus is that these adjustments don't cost much money. As water prices increase, performing inexpensive adjustments that save up to 30% of your water start to seem practical if not mandatory. Most of the changes recommended here will provide instant water savings with no additional costs, and they take little time. Let's look at a few of them.

Wet Checks

Almost every landscape maintenance contract has a section that covers a "wet check" of the irrigation system. The contracts often call for a monthly wet check; a few require a wet check after every mowing. The latter is preferable, simply because irrigation damage is often caused during mowing and maintenance with edgers or trimmers. Accidents and vandals also cause damage too. The sooner you can identify system problems, the sooner water waste can be corrected—to avoid unpleasant bills from your water company or seeping waste, more than a once-a-month wet check of the irrigation system is required.

A wet check of an irrigation system is just an evaluation process conducted while the irrigation system is running. It requires turning the system on, valve by valve, and observing what is happening. This lets you know whether any significant or minor issues need attention. The purpose of a wet check is to inspect and ensure that all irrigation system components are functioning correctly and efficiently. During a wet check, the following aspects are typically examined:

1 *Sprinkler Head Function:* Checking that all sprinkler heads pop up and retract properly, have the correct pressure, and are not blocked or damaged.

2 *Coverage Uniformity:* Ensuring the water is distributed evenly across the landscape without dry spots or over-saturated areas.

3 *Leaks and Breaks:* Identifying any leaks in the system, including those in valves, pipes, and sprinkler heads.

4 *Nozzle Performance:* Verifying nozzles produce the correct spray pattern and are not clogged or worn out.

5 *Pressure Issues:* Observe water pressure at various points in the system to ensure it's within the recommended range for optimal performance.

6 *Drainage:* Checking for proper drainage and no runoff or erosion issues.

All these are issues that could occur during routine maintenance and mowing. Mowing usually occurs once weekly—in, around, and over irrigation mechanisms. The risk of damaging the irrigation system is high. So after mowing is an excellent time to turn the system on to ensure it is functioning correctly.

The simple act of turning on your system and observing what's happening can reveal information about its current state. What might seem like a mundane task is, in fact, one of the most powerful tools in our water management arsenal. Understanding what to look for during these wet checks allows you to spot issues that, although seemingly minor, can cumulatively lead to substantial water loss.

Spotting and Fixing Leaks in Your Irrigation System

A common sight in any garden or landscape is the subtle emergence of silt and water bubbling up from the ground. This phenomenon often points to an issue within your irrigation system, potentially a loose connection where the sprinkler is threaded into the piping. It means the cover of the head is coming loose or a fitting is coming apart from the tubing. The solution might be as simple as tightening the sprinkler to its connection, but ignoring it could lead to more significant issues over time. Never ignore leaks in irrigation systems; they tend to escalate, eroding soil, creating holes, or damaging the landscape if left unaddressed.

However, not all wet spots are due to leaks. Sometimes, consistent wetness or a minor runoff can be traced back to a low-point drain in your system. These are signs that water's still escaping while your system is off. By way of gravity, the water pooling at the lowest spot in the system gradually leaks out of the system through the emission device. Everything is working correctly. It's just that the system is not perfectly level (not many are), and the water is leaking out. This is most visible on sloped landscapes. You can tell where it's occurring because the soil at the bottom is often wetter than the top. This is due to two issues. Gravity pulls water down the slope, and leaks form in the lowest emission devices. One of these you can resolve—the latter. One way to counteract this is by installing sprinklers with check valves, particularly at low points, to prevent water from draining out of the system when it's shut off. Check valves are open when the water pressure valve is open, and that when the main water

is shut off, they close. This way, all the water in the pipe does not drain out the end. This measure ensures that when your sprinklers come on, they're not wasting water by refilling the pipes and draining again after each cycle.

If you suspect a leak but cannot find it, one of the best ways to test for it is to check your water meter. See if the blue dial moves when all the water is off. If it's moving (or spinning), there is a leak. The blue or sometimes red triangle detects even the most minor of leaks. Finding the leak will be another issue, but at least you know you need to start looking for a problem point. Two key points are where the water meter and the water shutoff valve are located.

Typical Locations for a Water Meter

Outside the Home: The water meter is often located near the curb or sidewalk in front of the home, in a buried box usually marked "Water." It might also be on the side of the house.

Inside the Home: In colder climates, to prevent freezing, the meter might be located inside, often in a basement, crawl space, utility area, or garage.

Typical Locations for a Shutoff Valve

On the Property: The main shutoff valve is usually found near where the water line enters your house. Look for it along the foundation wall; it may be outside in warmer climates.

Inside the Home: In colder areas, the shutoff value could be inside to prevent freezing. Typically it'll be in a basement, utility room, or near the water heater. It may also be in a crawl space or garage.

Close to the Meter: The main shutoff valve is often near the meter. There could also be a customer valve on the house side of the meter that you can turn off.

Ask the Neighbors: If your homes were constructed at about the same time (say, in a subdivision), your neighbors may have their meters and shutoff valves in the same relative location as yours.

Contact Your Water Utility: If you're unable to locate your meter or shutoff valve, you can call your local water utility company. They can provide the location or send someone to show you where it is.

Remember, the main shutoff valve is a critical component in managing your home's water supply

Troubleshooting Leaks

Some leaks create water fountains that are easy to spot. Others may be slow leaks around sprinklers or small breaks in a pipe of supply tubing that are more challenging to identify. The landscape might offer some good clues. Below, you can see a water puddle in the landscape, which is indicative of a leak issue, and the other is a sign of overwatering where the grass in one contained area is getting much taller relative to the other grass in the landscape—because it's getting an excess of water.

Sprinkler Leaks

Pop-up sprinklers have screw caps. They often are loosened by weed whips. These start as slow, drip leaks and become a solid stream over time. That is an easy repair. Tighten the cap during a wet check, eliminate the wasted drips, and never let the issue get exacerbated by waiting until the crack in the cap is so big it blows off the cap entirely. Pop-up sprinklers also have screw-on nozzles. These blow off easily, but are more often removed by vandals. This is easy to catch and repair at the time of a wet check as well. Keep some extra nozzles on hand to fit your irrigation system for quick, easy, and affordable repair.

Leaking Valves

When valves don't close entirely, it's often due to debris being lodged under the diaphragm. This causes the valves to leak slowly and often create a situation like

Water puddle

Excessive growth around leaky spigot

this one. Removing and cleaning a diaphragm is easy. Usually, a few screws or nuts are on the top of the valve. Remove those and pull out the diaphragm. Clean the diaphragm with water and replace it, or better yet, purchase a replacement diaphragm and replace the old one with the new one—there may be microscopic cuts in it that you can't see. There are several other common issues with valves, including loose solenoids. This can be hand tightened for a quick, easy fix. Often the bleed screw is loose or was not tightened correctly after a manual bleed. This can also be quickly corrected with hand tightening. Another common problem is debris becoming lodged between the bonnet and the solenoid. You can easily remove the solenoid and spray it with water for a quick, easy solution.

Pressure Is Too High

Pressure regulators are a great way to keep the pressure of an irrigation system at optimal levels. Often, irrigation systems do not have regulators, but a simple adjustment to keep the pressure at a level that does not contribute to water waste will have a huge effect on your water usage. The easiest way to accomplish this is to:

1 Activate the valve with the controller.

2 Adjust the flow on the valve with the flow control handle.

3 Observe pressure reduction by looking at your emission devices.

Runoff of excess water

Pressure regulator

4 For example, turn the flow control handle down if watering with sprays until a dip in the water is observed. Once a visible reduction of pressure (by watching the water) is observed while the system is running, turn the flow control handle back one turn. This will slightly increase the pressure.

It's crucial to act as soon as you notice an early indicator of a leak. A slight silt deposit or persistent dampness can quickly escalate into a more significant problem. Puddling could be the result of a leaky valve, while the silt accumulation

How a Bleed Screw Works

A bleed screw is a component found in many irrigation valves, and it serves a specific purpose in the operation and maintenance of the irrigation system. The primary function of a bleed screw is to open the valve manually. When you turn or loosen the bleed screw, it allows a small amount of water to "bleed" out of the valve's upper chamber. This drop in pressure causes the diaphragm within the valve to open, allowing water to flow through the valve even if the solenoid (the electronic component that typically opens the valve) is not activated.

This manual operation is beneficial for testing, maintenance, or if there is an issue with the solenoid or electrical controls.

HOW TO MAINTAIN A BLEED SCREW:

Regular Checks: Periodically inspect the bleed screw to ensure it's not too loose or too tight. A bleed screw that is too loose may cause a small leak, while one that is too tight might not function properly when you need to operate the valve manually.

Cleaning: Dirt, debris, and mineral deposits can accumulate around the bleed screw, potentially causing it to stick or become difficult to turn. Regular cleaning can prevent this.

Lubrication: Occasionally, it may be necessary to lubricate the threads of the bleed screw to ensure smooth operation.

Tightening: After using the bleed screw to open the valve manually, ensure it is adequately tightened back to its original position to prevent leaks.

that leads to runoff could possibly be indicative of system neglect. In addition to water loss, this can also create slip hazards, especially as temperatures drop and water turns to ice.

The role of an irrigation system extends beyond just watering plants; it entails maintaining a level of responsibility for the safety and well-being of the community. For instance, ensuring that sidewalks are dry by morning is crucial in senior living communities to prevent slip-and-fall accidents. Adjusting irrigation schedules so that turf areas are watered earlier in the evening ensures sidewalks are safe for those early morning walks.

Leaks might also stem from internal valve issues, which might not be as apparent. Sometimes, the solenoids in valves might be slightly open, or manual bleed screws aren't fully closed after maintenance checks. A full valve box of water could indicate a leak through an available bleed screw. Understanding that these nuances are indicating there might be a problem are key to proactively keeping your system's components in good repair, and can mean the difference between a minor adjustment you can perform yourself and a costly repair.

Detecting irrigation issues is not always about spotting the obvious leaks; sometimes, it's about noticing the subtle misalignments and incorrect adjustments. For instance, the misadjusted nozzle on a rotor head can lead to overwatering in one area and dry spots in another. This common mistake happens when the maintenance is rushed, or the correct parts are not readily available. The temptation to make a quick fix by turning down a nozzle rather than replacing it with the right size can lead to inefficient watering and wasted resources.

What to Watch for Concerning Leaks

Continuous Dripping: If you notice water continually dripping or seeping from around the bleed screw, it might not be adequately tightened.

Damaged O-Ring: The bleed screw often has an O-ring or washer to prevent leaks. If this component is damaged or worn out, it may cause a leak even if the bleed screw is tightened correctly.

Corrosion or Damage: Over time, the bleed screw itself can become corroded or damaged. Inspect it for any signs of wear and replace it if necessary.

Improper Operation: If the valve does not open or close correctly when using the bleed screw, it could indicate an issue with the valve's diaphragm or other internal components.

Proper maintenance and regular inspection of the bleed screw are essential for the overall health of your irrigation system. It ensures you can manually control your valves, especially when the automated system fails as well as during routine checks and maintenance.

Understanding Nozzle Adjustments

Nozzle adjustments are critical in ensuring even water distribution. An incorrectly adjusted nozzle can cause overwatering in one area and dry spots in another. For example, changing the diffuser screw on the nozzle incorrectly could lead to a horizontal spread of water rather than a precise throw. This improper distribution can be rectified by selecting the proper nozzle and using the correct adjustment tools provided by the manufacturer.

Adjusting a nozzle on an irrigation spray head is crucial for maintaining an effective and efficient irrigation system. Here's a step-by-step guide on how to properly adjust a nozzle:

Identify the Type of Nozzle:

First, determine what type of nozzle is installed on your spray head. Common types include fixed spray nozzles, adjustable spray nozzles, and rotary nozzles. Each type has a different adjustment method.

Adjusting Fixed Spray Nozzles

Fixed spray nozzles have a predetermined spray pattern and range. The primary adjustment you can make is correctly aligning the spray pattern with the area you want to water.

Gently rotate the stem of the spray head to align the nozzle with the desired watering area.

Adjusting Adjustable Spray Nozzles

For adjustable nozzles, you can change the spray pattern and sometimes the range. To adjust the spray pattern, look for a screw or a ring at the top of the nozzle. By turning this screw or ring, you can increase or decrease the arc of the spray pattern. Some adjustable nozzles also allow you to change the radius (distance) of the spray. This is usually done with a screw on the top of the nozzle. Turning this screw clockwise typically reduces the spray distance, and turning counterclockwise increases it.

Adjusting Rotary Nozzles

Rotary nozzles, which rotate as they spray, often have adjustments for both arc and radius.

Use a small flathead screwdriver or a unique key (if provided by the manufacturer) to adjust the arc and radius according to the manufacturer's instructions.

Fine-Tuning Nozzles

Turn on the irrigation system to observe the spray pattern.

Make fine adjustments while the system is running to ensure the desired coverage.

Be careful not to overtighten adjustment screws, as this can damage the nozzle.

Understanding Head-to-Head Coverage

Head-to-head coverage in irrigation refers to a layout and design principle where the spray from each sprinkler head (or rotor) reaches the range of the adjacent sprinkler head, covering the entire area uniformly with water. This concept is crucial for efficient and effective irrigation systems. Here's a breakdown of what it means and why it's important:

Complete Coverage: Each sprinkler head should be positioned so that its spray reaches the outside arc of the neighboring sprinkler heads. The idea is that the edge of the water pattern from one sprinkler should overlap with the edge of the next sprinkler's pattern.

Uniform Distribution: This arrangement ensures that water is distributed uniformly across the lawn or garden. It helps avoid dry spots (areas that receive less water) and wet spots (areas that receive too much water).

Benefits of Head-to-Head Coverage:

Uniformity in Watering: Ensures that all parts of the landscape receive equal amounts of water, which is essential for the health and appearance of the lawn and plants.

Efficiency: Improves water use efficiency, reducing waste and potentially lowering water bills.

Prevention of Overwatering and Underwatering: Helps to prevent areas of overwatering and underwatering, which can be detrimental to plant health.

Adaptability to Various Conditions: Provides flexibility to adjust to different types of soil, slopes, and sun exposures by allowing for consistent moisture levels across different areas.

Try these simple irrigation maintenance hacks for the problems listed below before you call in an expensive repairman. You might surprise yourself with what you can fix yourself!

Broken Sprinkler Hopefully, at a minimum, you are inspecting your irrigation system monthly for broken heads. Try to inspect after every mowing. Broken heads waste tons of water, and everyone has a story of a broken head that resulted in a $40,000 water bill. A visual inspection is quick and easy to complete, and the results are gallons of water saved each time you spot an issue.

Regular Irrigation System Maintenance

Regularly check and clean nozzles to prevent clogging and ensure optimal performance.

Replace any nozzles that are damaged or showing signs of wear.

Adjusting a rotor (rotary sprinkler head) involves configuring its spray distance (radius) and the arc (the angle of the water spray). The exact method can vary depending on the brand and model, but here's a general guide for the two main adjustments:

TO ADJUST THE SPRAY DISTANCE (RADIUS):

Locate the Radius Adjustment Screw: This is typically found on top of the rotor head. It's usually a small screw that can be turned with a flathead screwdriver.

Make the Adjustment: To reduce the spray distance, turn the screw clockwise. This restricts the flow of water, thus shortening the radius.

To increase the distance, turn the screw counterclockwise. Be careful not to unscrew it completely.

Identify the Arc Adjustment Points: Most rotors have two adjustment points for setting the left and right stops of the arc. One side is generally fixed (usually the left), and the other side (usually the right) is adjustable.

Adjusting the Fixed Side (If Applicable): Some models allow adjustment of the fixed side by manually rotating the entire stem of the sprinkler to the desired starting point.

Adjusting the Adjustable Side: Use the rotor's special adjustment tool or a small flathead screwdriver, depending on the model.

Insert the tool into the arc adjustment socket, usually found on top of the rotor head.

Turn the tool clockwise to increase the arc or counterclockwise to decrease it.

Additional Tips: Check the manufacturer's instructions: Since different models and brands can vary significantly, it's important to refer to the specific instructions provided by the manufacturer.

Test and Observe: After making adjustments, run the system to observe the changes and ensure coverage is as desired.

Be Gentle: When making adjustments, do so gently to avoid damaging the rotor.

Regular Maintenance: Regularly check and clean the rotors to ensure they function correctly, especially after adjusting them.

Professional Help: If you are unsure about making adjustments, consulting a professional might be a good idea, especially for complex systems or large landscapes.

Misting Notice water misting everywhere when you turn the spray head sprinklers on? Usually, this is an issue that indicates you have the pressure set too high, on almost all occasions. Most spray heads should operate at 30 psi, and most irrigation systems have higher pressure than 30 psi. Regulating the pressure down at the sprinkler or the valve would be best. You can purchase pressure reducers or pressure-reducing sprinklers. This is typically easy and inexpensive to do. Often, this is the first and quickest modification to make to an existing system that provides the fastest return on investment.

Irrigation Running When It's Raining Many excellent wireless rain sensors are on the market today that can be purchased and installed for less than $200. These connect wirelessly to your controller and shut off irrigation at the slightest hint of rain so you don't duplicate effort with Mother Nature. This will keep you from getting those sideways looks from neighbors when your irrigation blasts while it's raining.

Runoff When water runs off your landscape because you are applying water too fast, a simple fix is to program your controller with multiple start times. For example, instead of watering for 9 minutes a day, try three different start times with 3-minute run times for a total of 9 minutes. Spread out these start times to allow water to soak into your landscape. Check if your controller has a cycle and soak feature built in. If it does, the cycle and soak feature will do this for you.

Mature Shrub Blocking Irrigation When a large plant blocks one of your irrigation emission points, it is a clear sign you need to switch to drip irrigation. You can prune your shrubs back, but typically, you won't like the look of the shrub because you will need to trim so much back to allow the water to spray up and out that you'll feel like the shrub looks butchered. Converting sprays or rotors to drip in this situation will save water and money and reduce the time you spend weeding in areas that receive water but have no plants.

Old Irrigation Controller Irrigation controllers older than five years are not utilizing current technology and are wasting water and money. Upgrade your controller to a new smart controller.

Drip Irrigation Hacks

Drip irrigation is the most efficient way to water your landscaping beds, vegetable gardens, and container plants. For non-grass areas like these, drip irrigation is an ideal watering solution, providing excellent results while also saving water. Below are some troubleshooting tips to help with your drip irrigation projects. These cover some of the most common issues with drip irrigation. Please remember most problems with drip irrigation are related to incorrect installation or improper usage of particular components.

Distribution Is Uneven

Check to see if emitter flow rates are mixed. Verify by checking the color code and flow rate. Next, check to see if too many emitters are hooked up to the supply line. Depending on the line size, you are limited in the number of emitters. Is the supply pressure less than 5 PSI or more than 45 PSI? Next, check to see if the emitters are clogged. If the emitters are blowing off the tubing, check to ensure you are using a pressure reducer.

Micro-Irrigation System Spray

If your micro head is not performing up to standards, consider these:

- Tubing supply pressure is too low or too great. Pressure should be 10–20 psi.

- The supply tubing is kinked.

- The filter is clogged.

- The spray head is clogged with debris and needs cleaning.

- Supply tubing is run too far from the point of connection, or too many spray heads are used for the size of polyethylene tubing. (Pinch supply tubing at the halfway point and check performance).

¼-Inch Dripline Tubing Problems
If Your Mini Pipeline Is Distributing Water Unevenly:

- Supply pressure incorrect. It should be 6-20 psi.

- Lateral run length exceeds recommendations.

- Tubing is clogged. Clean or replace and add a 150 mesh filter.

- Lateral lines are running uphill rather than sidehill or downhill.

- Lateral lines are greater than 12 inches apart.

If Your ¼-Inch Dripline Is Emitting Water Unevenly:

- The line length exceeds the manufacturer's recommendations for the bubbler flow rate.

- Tubing is kinked.

- Tubing is clogged; clean or replace, and consider adding a 150 mesh filter.

Bubbler Watering System

If Tubing Blows off Bubbler Port, Check to See If:

- Tubing is kinked.
- Insect plug is inserted too far.
- Emitters have been inserted into the end of the bubbler tubing.
- Tubing is in a high-traffic area and requires a clamp plate.
- Tubing has been pulled off the bubbler too many times. Cut one inch off the end and reinsert.
- Improper tubing size is being used.

If Bubbler Ports have Uneven Flows, It May Be That:

- Bubbler's flow path is partially clogged with debris. Remove the screen and diaphragm to clean the flow path notch.
- The system filter is plugged in.

These are only some challenges found, but they cover the 80/20 rule well. Congratulations on watering with the most efficient irrigation available today. Matching drip irrigation with a smart controller, saving water, and having a healthy landscape will be simple.

Irrigation System Optimization Checklist

Regularly inspect your irrigation system as part of your gardening routine, and you will be repaid with lower water bills and a more beautiful garden.

Pressure Regulation:

- Check the current pressure of your system using a pressure gauge.
- Compare the measured pressure against the optimal operating pressure for your system.
- Adjust the flow control on the valve to achieve the desired pressure, reducing leaks and misting.

Nozzle Adjustments:

- Inspect each nozzle to ensure the intended area is the correct type and size.
- Use manufacturer-provided tools to adjust the arc and distance of the nozzles.
- Replace incorrectly sized nozzles with ones that match the zone's requirements.

System Leak Checks:

- Conduct visual inspections for signs of leaks, such as silt or constant wet areas.
- Tighten any loose connections and/or replace damaged sprinkler heads.
- If persistent leaks are found, consider replacing the valve diaphragm or the entire valve, if necessary.

Smart Controller Setup:

- Install a smart controller with a flow sensor to monitor and adjust water usage.
- Program the controller according to the specific watering needs of each zone.
- Regularly update the controller's settings to reflect changes in weather and landscape needs.

Manual Pressure Checks:

- Perform regular manual checks to verify the system's operating pressure.
- Use hose-bib pressure gauges or sprinkler-mounted gauges for accurate readings.
- Adjust the pressure accordingly to maintain efficiency and prevent wastage.

Sprinkler Head Inspection:

- Ensure sprinkler heads are not damaged or obstructed.
- Check for proper spray patterns and adjust as needed to cover the designated areas without overspray.
- Clean or replace any clogged nozzles and filters.

Water Usage Analysis:

- Review water usage data from the smart controller or water meter readings.
- Look for anomalies that suggest leaks or overuse.
- Implement adjustments or repairs based on your findings.

Efficiency Audit:

- Consider conducting a professional water audit to determine the system's efficiency.
- Utilize the audit results to make targeted adjustments to the system.
- Repeat the audit periodically or after significant changes to the landscape or system.

Seasonal Adjustments:

- Adjust watering schedules seasonally to account for changes in temperature and precipitation.
- Reduce watering in cooler months and increase as needed during hotter periods, always considering local weather data.

Safety Considerations:

- Ensure sidewalks and pathways are clear of overspray to prevent slip hazards.
- Adjust watering times to avoid freezing conditions that could create ice.

Pressure and Nozzle Chart Review:

- Refer to the manufacturer's charts to understand the relationship between nozzle size, pressure, and GPM.
- Select nozzles and adjust the pressure to achieve the desired irrigation coverage without excess misting or runoff.

Final System Check:

- After making adjustments, run the system to ensure everything operates as intended.
- Observe each zone's performance, noting any further adjustments needed.
- Document any changes made for future reference and maintenance.
- By systematically following this checklist, you can ensure that your irrigation system operates at peak efficiency, providing the necessary water to your landscape while minimizing waste and reducing costs.

10

Common Irrigation Issues and Simple Fixes

MOST HOMEOWNERS NEED THE HELP of professionals to install an irrigation system. However, once the system is installed, there are many maintenance functions homeowners can perform themselves to make their irrigation systems run more efficiently. This chapter will explain most homeowners' typical irrigation issues and how to fix them.

Landscape irrigation issues often involve system design, maintenance challenges, and environmental factors. Addressing these issues is crucial for ensuring efficient water use and maintaining a healthy landscape. Here are some of the most prevalent problems.

Uneven coverage in sprinkler irrigation systems occurs when water is not uniformly distributed over the landscaped area, resulting in some sections receiving too much water while others receive too little. This inconsistency can be due to various factors, including improperly spaced sprinkler heads, varying water pressures, obstructions that block water flow, or sprinklers unsuitable for the area they're supposed to water. The issue of uneven coverage is significant because it directly affects the health and appearance of the landscape. Overwatered areas can lead to waterlogged soil, promoting root rot, fungus, and diseases, while underwatered areas can result in dry spots where grass and plants struggle to survive and grow. This can create a patchy, unhealthy landscape that requires more maintenance and can be more susceptible to weed invasion.

Uneven coverage is not only a problem for plant health but also for water conservation efforts. Overwatering certain areas to ensure dry spots receive sufficient water leads to significant water waste—both environmentally unfriendly and costly. Additionally, excess water runoff from overwatered areas can carry fertilizers and pesticides into the local water system, contributing to pollution and eutrophication in nearby bodies of water.

The first step to fix uneven coverage is visually inspecting the irrigation system. This involves checking for broken or clogged sprinkler heads, ensuring they are correctly positioned, and assessing whether the pressure is adequate for each zone. Replacing mismatched or damaged sprinkler heads, adjusting the watering schedule, and cleaning out any debris that might obstruct the flow are immediate measures to improve coverage. Additionally, consider repositioning sprinkler heads to eliminate gaps in the watering pattern and ensure that each head is spraying in the correct arc and radius.

Sprinklers throwing water less than normal, falling short: The nozzle or filter is clogged. To correct this problem, unscrew the nozzle when the system is off and rinse the nozzle and filter. It's easy to fill a bucket with water and rinse each nozzle and filter at the location of installation. This is a quick and easy solution for uneven coverage.

The spray head is not level: Make sure the spray head is not tilted up or down.

Spray body and head have settled into the ground: Dig around the spray body and try to raise it. If that does not work, purchase a taller spray head. These are usually sold in 3″, 4″, 6″, and 12″ heights.

Indicators the system is leaking: When inspecting the irrigation system, check for these issues: A loose cap will leak water under pressure. Tighten the cap by hand when you see this issue. A loose nozzle will also leak water under pressure. The nozzles are often threaded onto the stem, and you can twist these on or off with your hands. Sometimes, you may need some pliers to tighten or loosen them. A clogged filter or nozzle will also cause misting in your system. When this occurs, much of the water evaporates into the air because the water molecules are too small. Rinsing the nozzle and filter will help with this as well.

No water spraying from the sprinkler: Check if the nozzle is adjustable. If it is, ensure the pattern is not set to zero and adjust to the correct pattern. The other cause is a clogged filter or nozzle. Please clean as recommended above.

The spray is not a full pattern: If the sprinkler has a gap in the middle of the pattern or does not reach the sides the way it did in the past, you may have to adjust the pattern. A clogged nozzle or filter causes this as well. Sometimes, the pattern is not adjusted correctly, and the nozzle needs to be threaded to improve the pattern.

Adjusting a Spray Head Sprinkler

Adjusting a spray head sprinkler involves tweaking its spray pattern, distance, and direction to ensure optimal coverage of your lawn or garden area. Here's a simple guide on how to adjust a typical spray head sprinkler.

You'll need a flathead screwdriver and sometimes a special adjustment key or tool, depending on the sprinkler model.

Identify the type of spray head: Understand the brand and model of your spray head sprinkler, as different models might have slightly different adjustment methods. Common brands include Hunter, Orbit, Rain Bird, and Toro.

Adjust the spray pattern (arc): Many spray head sprinklers are fixed-pattern types, meaning they're designed to spray water in a set pattern (like quarter-circle, half-circle, or full-circle). The pattern is usually indicated on the nozzle.

If you have an adjustable pattern spray head, you can change the pattern by rotating the collar on the nozzle. Turn it to align with the area you want to water. This is typically done by hand, without tools.

Set the spray distance (radius): To adjust the distance the water is thrown, look for the screw located on top of the nozzle. Using a flathead screwdriver, turn this screw clockwise to decrease the spray distance or counterclockwise to increase it. Adjusting this screw changes the flow rate, which in turn adjusts the distance. Reducing or increasing the throw by a foot or two is acceptable. Any distance greater than a foot or two requires a new nozzle with a shorter or longer throw.

Adjust the spray direction: For fixed spray heads, the entire head, including the body and nozzle, may need to be rotated to change the direction of the spray. This is done by manually turning the stem or the body of the sprinkler. Ensure the sprinkler is adjusted to cover the desired area without spraying onto sidewalks, buildings, or roads.

Check for even coverage: Once adjustments are made, run the irrigation system to observe the spray pattern and coverage. Look for any dry spots or areas of overlap and adjust as necessary.

Fine-tuning: Make small incremental adjustments to achieve the desired coverage. It may take a few tries to get it right.

Important Tips

Avoid over tightening: When adjusting the spray distance screw, be careful not to overtighten it, as it can damage the nozzle.

Conduct regular maintenance: Inspect and clean the nozzles to prevent clogging from dirt or debris.

Properly adjusting your spray head sprinklers can lead to more efficient water use and a healthier lawn or garden. Find that your adjustments are not giving you the coverage you need? It might be necessary to reevaluate the placement of your sprinklers or consult with a landscape or irrigation professional.

Adjusting a Rotor Sprinkler

Adjusting an irrigation rotor sprinkler is a task that can be done relatively quickly. Still, it requires careful attention to detail to ensure proper coverage and efficient water use. Here's a step-by-step guide on how to adjust rotor sprinklers.

You'll need a flathead screwdriver or a rotor adjustment tool (specific to the brand/model of your rotor) and a tape measure (optional, for measuring spray distance).

Identify the type of rotor sprinkler: Different brands and models of rotor sprinklers have slightly different adjustment methods. Familiarize yourself with your specific model. Common brands include Hunter, Rain Bird, and Toro.

Adjust the spray distance (arc): Most rotor sprinklers have an adjustment screw on top that controls the spray distance or radius. Using a flathead screwdriver, turn the screw clockwise to decrease the spray distance or counterclockwise to increase it. Be cautious not to overtighten the screw, as this can damage the sprinkler.

Set the rotation limits (arc adjustment): Rotor sprinklers typically cover an area in an arc ranging from 40 to 360 degrees. Look for adjustment points on the sprinkler head, usually small plus and minus signs. Insert the screwdriver into the adjustment socket. Turn it toward the plus sign to increase the arc or the minus sign to decrease it. Some models require lifting the sprinkler riser and manually rotating the turret to the desired start and end points.

Adjust the spray pattern: If your sprinkler allows pattern adjustment, you can tweak it to ensure even coverage. This usually involves rotating the head or a part of the nozzle to align with the desired area.

Check for head-to-head coverage: Ensure that the spray from each rotor head reaches the adjacent heads. This provides uniform coverage and prevents dry spots.

Test the sprinkler: Run your irrigation system to observe the adjustments. Make additional adjustments if areas need more water.

Fine-tuning: Make minor adjustments as needed and observe the changes. Measure the spray distance with a tape measure if precise adjustments are required.

Important Tips

Understand the limits: Each sprinkler model has a maximum and minimum adjustment range. Avoid forcing the sprinkler beyond these limits to prevent damage.

Conduct regular maintenance: Check your rotor sprinklers for debris or damage, especially after mowing or significant weather events.

Follow manufacturer's instructions: Refer to the manufacturer's instructions or website for specific guidance on your sprinkler model.

Adjusting rotor sprinklers is about balancing the needs of your landscape with water conservation. Proper adjustment ensures that your lawn and garden receive adequate water without waste. Contact a professional for assistance if you need clarification or are uncomfortable making these adjustments yourself.

Troubleshooting

The spray head gets stuck in the up position or does not pop up all the way: This is often caused by debris or grit getting stuck between the spray body and stem. Try holding the spray down for a minute while the system is running. If that does not fix the problem, untwist the cap and rinse the debris or grit from the stem.

Matched precipitation rate: This is a term you often encounter, especially when discussing sprinkler heads and nozzles. The "matched precipitation rate" concept is pivotal for someone just beginning to understand irrigation. Matched precipitation rate refers to the rate at which water is applied uniformly across a specific area by an irrigation system. It's measured in inches per hour (in/hr) and ensures that every part of the landscaped area receives the same amount of water over the same period. This concept is crucial because it prevents landscape areas from getting too much or too little water, ensuring each plant receives the necessary moisture for optimal growth.

One common mistake beginners make is mixing different types of sprinklers within the same irrigation zone. Sprinklers vary in precipitation rates; for example, spray heads and rotors deliver water at different rates. When mixed in the same zone, achieving a uniform application rate across the entire area becomes challenging. Some parts of the landscape will receive too much water while others will receive too little, leading to inefficient irrigation and potentially harming the health of the plants.

To avoid these problems, using the same type of sprinkler with the same precipitation rate throughout a single zone is vital. This consistency allows for more accurate control of the amount of water applied and ensures each part of the zone receives equal water. It simplifies setting up your irrigation schedule, as you can calculate a single watering duration that suits the entire zone.

This concept is integral to understanding how an efficient irrigation system functions. Precipitation rate is the speed at which sprinklers apply water to their designated area, typically expressed in inches per hour. When we talk about a matched precipitation rate, it means that all sprinkler heads watering a specific area proportionally apply water.

So, why is this crucial? The primary objective when designing an irrigation system is to ensure the uniform distribution of water across an area, irrespective of its shape or size. Achieving this uniformity involves a combination of factors, including the correct water volume and pressure, matched precipitation rate nozzles, and head-to-head coverage. This means the water from each head should reach the adjacent heads to ensure no part of the turf is left dry or receives too little water. If the precipitation rates of the sprinklers do not match, it results in certain areas being either overwatered or underwatered.

To rectify this imbalance, sprinkler run times are often adjusted at the irrigation controller. However, this makeshift solution doesn't truly address the problem; it merely shifts the issue, causing other adequately watered areas to become flooded or dry out. Modern spray head nozzles, like those from Rain Bird, often have matched precipitation rates within the same product line and radius. For instance, a Rain Bird 15′ MPR nozzle maintains a consistent precipitation rate across all arc degrees. Whether it's a quarter, half, or full circle spray at 30 psi, each arc will deliver water at 1.58 inches per hour. The key is the same amount of water, even though the area the water hits may be larger or smaller.

Addressing odd-shaped bedding areas requires extra effort to achieve head-to-head coverage while maintaining a matched precipitation rate. This might involve using a mix of nozzles with varying radii, which can be challenging as standard spray nozzles often have different precipitation rates for each radius. A solution is to use nozzles with matched precipitation rates across all distances. For example, Hunter's MP Rotator nozzles offer a matched precipitation rate of 0.4 inches per hour for their MP1000, MP2000, and MP3000 series across all arcs and radii. However, it's important to note that the MP Rotator's rate is significantly lower than standard spray head nozzles, so you must increase zone run times accordingly. For larger turf areas that use rotors, brands like Rain Bird and Hunter now provide matched precipitation rate nozzles for specific models, including Rain Bird's 5000 series and Hunter's PGP Ultra and I-20 rotors.

Understanding and implementing matched precipitation rates in your irrigation system is fundamental for any beginner. It ensures uniform water distribution, promotes plant health, conserves water, and saves money. Avoid mixing different types of sprinklers within the same zone to maintain this uniformity. With careful planning and consideration of matched precipitation rates, you can create an efficient and effective irrigation system to keep your landscape thriving while conserving water resources.

Proactive Considerations for Managing Wasteful Runoff

If the irrigation system applies water faster than the soil can absorb it or if slopes are not managed correctly, runoff can occur, leading to erosion and wasted water. Solving runoff issues in your landscape, especially those caused by sprinkler system problems, involves a combination of proper system design, appropriate scheduling, and landscape management. Here are steps to address and prevent runoff:

Install pressure-regulating devices: High pressure can cause misting, leading to uneven coverage and runoff. Installing pressure-regulating devices ensures that sprinklers operate at the optimal pressure.

Use appropriate sprinkler heads: Employ sprinkler heads that are appropriate for the area's size and shape. For example, use rotors for large, open areas and drip irrigation for smaller or densely planted areas.

Optimize watering schedules: Implement the "cycle and soak" method. Instead of watering continuously for a long period, break the watering time into shorter cycles. This allows water to soak into the soil before more is applied, reducing runoff.

Aerate lawns: Aerating your lawn creates holes in the soil, improves water infiltration, and reduces runoff.

Add organic matter: Incorporating compost or other organic matter into the soil can enhance its water-holding capacity and structure, reducing runoff.

Practice regular maintenance: Lack of regular maintenance can lead to various problems, such as leaks going undetected, clogged nozzles not being cleaned, and system updates not being made in response to changing landscape needs.

Monitor pressure: Too much pressure can cause misting, which leads to evaporation and wind drift, while too little pressure can result in inadequate coverage.

Consider your soil type: Different soil types have different water infiltration rates. If the irrigation system doesn't account for this, it can lead to rapid runoff or waterlogging.

Monitor weather: Without sensors or smart controllers that adjust to current weather conditions, systems can waste water by running in the rain or failing to provide extra water during drought conditions.

Use the correct irrigation method: Using sprinklers for plants that benefit more from drip irrigation (or vice versa) can lead to inefficiencies and plant health issues.

Know your climate: Not adjusting irrigation practices to account for seasonal and climate variations can result in inadequate watering and increased water use without benefitting the landscape.

Addressing common irrigation problems doesn't always require professional help; many homeowners can make these adjustments themselves. By routinely inspecting and cleaning sprinkler heads, ensuring they're correctly aligned and leveled, and adjusting the spray pattern and distance, you can significantly improve your system's efficiency and curb runoff issues. Employing matched precipitation rate nozzles and adjusting watering schedules according to the actual needs of your landscape can also mitigate overwatering. These straightforward fixes not only help conserve water but also enhance the health of your garden, all while avoiding the cost of professional intervention. Remember, the most effective irrigation system is one that's regularly monitored and finely tuned to the unique contours and requirements of your own landscape.

11

Drip Irrigation Best Practices

BACK IN THE EIGHTIES AND NINETIES, home builders pumped out houses as fast as possible. Some home builders were pushed to construct as many as 30 homes per day in places like Southern California. This meant they could only install quick, simple irrigation systems that sprayed water everywhere. The designs did not focus on efficient irrigation. They were designed for quick installations. Many of those irrigations systems are still being used, but we need to improve on them.

Water conservation stands out as the primary advantage of what today we call micro-irrigation systems. Very little micro-irrigation was used in past decades, but fortunately, most homeowners whose properties are plumbed for simple irrigation systems can convert them to micro systems or create irrigation zones for drip irrigation.

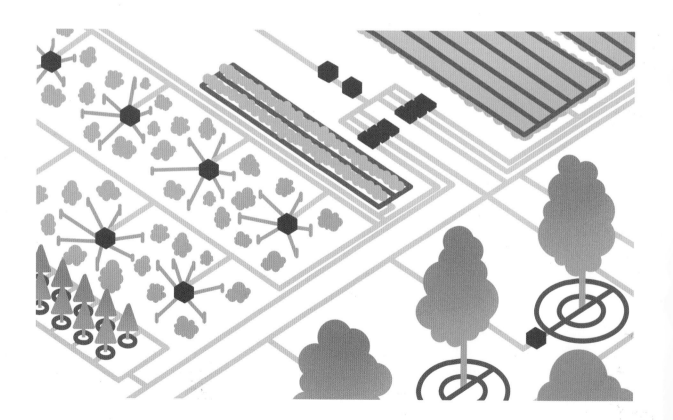

Benefits of Micro-Irrigation

Micro-irrigation systems are designed with low application rates in mind, making them ideal for delivering water slowly over an extended period, typically 1 to 2 hours. This slow delivery system, utilizing polyethylene emitter tubing or micro-sprinklers, ensures that water is directly supplied to the plants or uniformly covers areas with closely spaced plantings. A significant advantage of these systems is their flexibility; it's relatively simple to adjust the number and positions of emitters or micro-sprinklers in response to changes in the landscape or plant growth patterns.

Typically, micro-irrigation systems are designed to deliver water at a slow and steady rate, ranging from 0.5 to 2 gallons per hour (gph) per emitter for drip systems. This low flow rate ensures water is applied directly to the plant's root zone, with minimal waste. However, the total water delivery capacity of the system over a given area depends on the number of emitters and their spacing, as well as the system's operating pressure and the duration the system runs. The maximum amount of water a micro-irrigation system can deliver is determined by several factors, including the capacity of the water source, the size and design of the irrigation system, and the specific components used, such as the type of emitters (drippers, micro-sprayers, or bubblers) and their flow rates.

While there isn't a fixed "maximum" amount of water these systems can deliver—because it varies widely based on design and setup—micro-irrigation systems are generally not intended for applications requiring high volumes of water delivered quickly. Instead, they are optimized for efficiency and precision, providing enough water for plant health without overwatering. For larger landscapes or agricultural areas, the system might be scaled up with more lines and emitters to cover more ground, still adhering to the principles of delivering water directly to the root zone of each plant.

These systems allow us to use water, our most valuable natural asset, with unparalleled efficiency. A well-planned, installed, and maintained micro-irrigation setup surpasses any other irrigation method to promote healthy plants, improve soil conditions, and maximize resource use.

Micro-irrigation systems deliver water directly to plants, catering to their unique water needs. These systems can save up to 70% more water than traditional irrigation methods. They achieve this by watering plants at very low rates, significantly reducing water loss due to wind, evaporation, runoff from sloped landscapes, and other external factors.

One of the key strengths of micro-irrigation is its ability to target water directly to the root zone—the area where plants absorb most of their nutrients. This targeted watering produces robust roots, resulting in healthier and more resilient plants. Additionally, micro-irrigation avoids delivering water to non-plant areas, reducing the risk of accidents in high-foot-traffic zones and preventing water damage to fences, buildings, or paved areas.

System Considerations

Micro irrigation setups can be designed from scratch for new landscapes or integrated into existing sprinkler systems to enhance water conservation. Knowing the type of system you have guides the design process and aids in selecting the right components.

Deciding if you need devices to manage water pressure and flow for micro-irrigation is essential. This decision depends on various factors, such as the landscape's slope, the size and shape of the watered area, and the number of water connection points. In landscapes with uneven terrain or large areas to cover, pressure-compensating devices are recommended to ensure even watering despite long tubing distances. However, most home gardens are smaller and can be efficiently watered with more straightforward, turbulent flow devices, as long as there's proper pressure regulation.

Homeowners can significantly reduce water usage by opting for micro-irrigation while supporting lush, healthy plant growth and contributing to environmental sustainability.

Creating a detailed landscape plan is a critical step toward designing an efficient irrigation system tailored to the specific needs of your yard and plants. Here's a structured approach to drafting your landscape plan and planning your irrigation system:

Drafting Your Landscape Plan

Sketch the Layout: Begin with a rough sketch of your yard. Include the house, driveway, walkways, trees, garden beds, and other significant features. While precision is helpful, the goal is to create a workable outline of your space.

Identify Planting Areas: Mark the locations of all planting areas, distinguishing between lawn spaces, flower beds, vegetable gardens, and any trees or shrubs.

Catalog Plant Types and Sizes: Note the types of plants in each area and their sizes or the expected sizes of new plantings. This information is crucial for determining water needs.

Water Sources and Existing Irrigation: Indicate the location of fixtures, water lines, and any existing irrigation components. This helps in planning the layout of the new irrigation system.

Water Requirements: Assess the water needs of each plant or area. This could range from high, medium, to low water use, influencing your irrigation design.

Planning Your Irrigation System

Determine Available Pressure: Most irrigation devices, such as bubblers, emitters, and spray systems, operate efficiently between 20–30 psi at the head. Verify that your water source can provide at least 30 psi to ensure adequate flow. Utilize a pressure test kit to measure and plot your system's pressure, aiding in the design and determining the need for pressure regulators.

Assess Filtration Needs: To prevent clogging of emission devices, it's essential to filter out rust, sand, and other particles from your water supply. The sensitivity to clogging varies with the device's flow rate; devices with lower flow rates require finer filtration.

Know Your Soil: Understanding your soil's water absorption and retention capabilities is crucial when designing an irrigation system for different soil types. For clay or sloping soils, high-application-rate systems like bubblers can lead to water runoff, missing the intended areas for watering. Low-flow emitters are a perfect choice for these situations. They typically run from 0.5 gallons per hour to 2 gallons per hour.

Determine the Zones of Your Irrigation System: The hotter areas in direct sunlight or surrounded by pavement should be separated from cooler, shaded areas. Seasonal-use garden areas should have their own zones. A grouping of potted plants should be zoned separately. Whatever makes it easier to manage the irrigation schedule in breaking down the landscape into zones of similar water utilization is always a good idea. These zones are called hydrozones.

Determine the Flow Rate Required in Each Zone: Add up the flow rates for each emitter or bubbler outlet and each micro-sprinkler in the zone. Divide this quantity by 60 to get the zone's flow rate in gallons per minute.

Calculate the Amount of Water Available: A given supply line will have a limit on the water available. To determine your water requirements, add up the flow rates of all bubbler outlets and divide by 60 to arrive at gallons per minute. The chart to the right will assist you in determining the number of stations or zones needed to service your system.

System Basics

Every low-volume irrigation system has basic requirements to function efficiently and effectively. Among these are a point of connection, backflow prevention, proper filtration, and pressure regulation. Low-volume irrigation systems employ very small pathways and discharge ports to apply water at a plant's required rate-usually 0.5 gallon per hour (GPH), 1 GPH, or 2 GPH. This varies from standard irrigation/spray head systems, which have larger flow paths and discharge water in gallons per minute (GPM). For these reasons, it is essential to keep the system free from debris and to regulate the pressure within the appropriate range of the chosen emission device.

Point of Connection

The first component of a micro irrigation system is the control valve. There are many makes and styles available. It is best to choose the valve size after you have a good idea of the total flow requirement for each zone. A valve that is oversized for the flow rate will have difficulty closing. A 1″ valve requires a minimum flow rate of 5 to 10 GPM; 5 GPM represents 300 1-GPH emitters.

There are two different standard points of connection (POC) in a micro-irrigation system:

1 Hose Bib (outside faucet) or Garden Valve Connection from which an adapter can be attached, initiating the system either electronically or manually.

2 Valve Connection may have been professionally installed utilizing underground piping to feed various watering zones.

Reference local code for valve requirements

Backflow Prevention

A backflow prevention device is required on all irrigation systems. If the valve you choose does not have a built-in anti-siphon device, or if a hose bib will be the valve controlling your new system, you should install an anti-siphon device on your system. This device is installed just before or after the valve and before the filter and regulator.

Filters and Filtration

The filter is one of the most critical components of a drip system. The filter traps all particles larger than the emitter pathways and prevents severe problems from plugged emitters. A 150-mesh screen will provide the best protection for your investment. Remember to check and clean your filter regularly. There are filters for different types of connections, depending on whether you are using a hose bib, garden hose, or professional/valve connection.

Y-filters range in size from ¾″ to 2″ and are available with flow ranges from 9 GPM to 100 GPM.

In-line filters are generally used where city water is the primary water source and is relatively free from debris. They contain mesh poly screens, which can be cleaned quickly and removed when not in service.

Plastic hose thread T-filters are attached to a hose bib (outside faucet). They are available with various replaceable stainless steel screens (50 mesh to 200 mesh) depending on water quality and levels of debris present. The screen is removable for periodic cleaning, and the T-filter is available with auto flush to reduce maintenance requirements.

Pressure Regulation

Pressure regulators are installed after the filter and are designed to reduce available water pressure to the appropriate operating range of the system. Many water sources need more pressure for efficient operation of low-volume systems. For most homes, the water pressure will be over 60 psi. Most micro-irrigation systems operate best between 20 and 30 psi.

Using a pressure regulator on your micro-irrigation system is crucial for several reasons, all of which contribute to your irrigation setup's efficiency, longevity, and effectiveness.

Optimizing Performance: A pressure regulator ensures the system receives water at this optimal pressure, essential for uniform water distribution. Without regulated pressure, water could be delivered more forcefully, leading to uneven irrigation and potentially harming plants.

Preventing Damage: High water pressure can cause significant wear and tear on irrigation components, leading to leaks, blowouts, and the premature failure of emitters and tubing. A pressure regulator protects your system by preventing excessive force that can damage these delicate components, thereby extending the lifespan of your irrigation system.

The size of the pressure regulator you should use on your micro irrigation system depends on a few key factors: the flow rate of your system, the incoming water pressure, and the optimal operating pressure for your irrigation components. Here's how to determine the correct size:

Determining the Flow Rate: Check the total flow rate of your irrigation system, measured in gallons per minute (GPM) or liters per hour (L/hr). This is the sum of the flow rates of all emitters or drippers in your system operating simultaneously.

Measure Your Incoming Water Pressure: Measure the static water pressure in your system without any water flowing. This can be done using a water pressure gauge attached to a faucet or valve on the same line as your irrigation system. The pressure is typically measured in pounds per square inch (psi).

Optimize Operating Pressure: Refer to the manufacturer's specifications for your irrigation components to find the recommended operating pressure. Most micro-irrigation systems, including drip systems, operate best at 20–30 psi.

Based on these factors, select a pressure regulator that can handle the flow rate of your system at the incoming water pressure and reduce it to the optimal operating pressure. Pressure regulators are often categorized by their inlet (maximum handling) pressure and outlet (regulated) pressure range. They come in different sizes, typically corresponding to the pipe size they'll be connected to (e.g. 1 inch, 1 inch).

For example:

- If your system has a flow rate of 5 GPM and your incoming water pressure is 60 psi, with an optimal operating pressure of 25 psi for your emitters, you'll need a pressure regulator that can reduce 60 psi to 25 psi at a flow rate of 5 GPM.

- If you're connecting the regulator directly to a standard garden hose or a 1/2-inch irrigation line, a 1/2-inch pressure regulator designed for the above specifications would be appropriate.

- It's also important to note that pressure regulators have a maximum pressure rating. Ensure the regulator you choose can handle the maximum pressure that may be present in your system to avoid damage.

Choosing the correct size pressure regulator is crucial for the efficiency and longevity of your micro-irrigation system. When in doubt, consult with a professional or refer to the guidelines provided by the irrigation equipment manufacturer to make sure you select a regulator that fits your system's specific needs.

Supply Tubing

The most common method of transporting the irrigation water to the planted areas is 17mm polyethylene tubing, also known as ½ inch tubing. This is facilitated by rolling the tubing out and placing it throughout the planted area. Several tubing sections can be laid out in sparsely planted areas using tees, elbows, and end caps.

When all the tubing is laid out, the system should be turned on and flushed before installing emitters.

When a drip system is far from the water supply, PVC pipe can be used to transport the water to the planted area.

Supply tubing can be installed above ground, below ground, or covered with landscaping material for a less conspicuous installation. Tubing is available in 100, 250, 500, and 1000 coils.

Micro-distribution tubing moves water from the main supply tubing to plant locations and emission devices through smaller distribution tubing, typically ⅛″ or ¼″, and manufactured from polyethylene or vinyl. Distribution tubing is attached via connectors punched directly into the supply tubing using a punch tool. From the primary supply tubing connection, micro-distribution tubing is easily run to various plant and emitter locations through tees, couplers, and elbows.

Fittings and Connectors

Low-volume irrigation fittings and connectors come in a variety of sizes and configurations. The most common fittings for micro-distribution tubing are ⅛″ or ¼″, barb and 10–32 thread fittings. These small fittings generally come in standard configurations: adapters, tees, elbows, and couplings.

Insert fittings have been the industry standard for a long time. Priced very economically and easy to use, 17mm insert fittings, in particular, are the go-to fitting of choice for contractors. Dual barb design keeps the emitter line on the fitting after the system becomes pressurized.

Power-Loc ™ fittings are the latest innovation in fittings, solving the problem of multiple fittings for multiple tubing sizes. The Power-Loc 55 Series is a multiple-tubing-size fitting, bringing the newest manufacturing technology together with field-proven experience. Power-Loc55s fit all standard ½″ Supply Tubing (.520–.620 inside diamteter), are fully customizable to fit any inlet/outlet requirement, and are reusable for line alteration or replacement. Supply tubing is placed on the Power-Loc barb, and the locking nut is tightened over the supply tubing, providing a secure seal from inside and outside the tubing.

Emission devices are the final component of every low-volume irrigation system. There are several emission devices to choose from, and the type needed will vary depending on each installation. Three basic low-volume irrigation systems exist: bubbler, drip, and micro-spray. All three types of systems are used for different applications and use different emission styles. Bubblers utilize higher flow and application rates, making bubbler systems an excellent method to retrofit conventional spray systems.

Dripline comes in various sizes, including ¼″ tubing with built-in ½ GPH in-line turbulent flow emitters at 6″ or 12″ spacings. It is ideal for use in vegetable gardens, densely planted ground cover, and for ringing trees and

shrubs. Quarter-inch dripline (available in black and brown) can be installed above ground or under mulch, eliminating wet walks and discoloring of decorative bark, fences, and windows. Output is approximately 0.5 gallon per outlet per hour. This is ideal for gardens, closely spaced plantings, and ground cover areas. Up to 30 feet of ¼″ can be used with each lateral line. Because the tubing is just ¼″, you can't run more than 30 feet. You will run out of water.

Half-inch or 17mm polyethylene tubing with built-in pressure compensating emitters (0.5, 1 GPH). These emitters are bonded inside the tubing

Maximum Recommended Emitterline on Level Ground (ft)

Inlet Pressure* psi	EMITTER FLOW RATE 0.5 GPH Emitter Spacing (in)			
	12″	18″	24″	36″
20	213	333	426	597
25	266	383	492	690
30	293	423	544	765
35	317	456	588	825
40	337	486	626	882
45	355	513	680	930
45	372	537	692	975

Inlet Pressure* psi	EMITTER FLOW RATE 1 GPH Emitter Spacing (in)			
	12″	18″	24″	36″
20	151	218	280	395
25	174	251	322	453
30	192	278	356	501
35	207	299	386	543
40	220	318	410	579
45	232	336	432	612
45	243	351	454	642

during extrusion and are spaced at 12″, 18″, or 24″ intervals. Dripline is common in narrow planting areas, under ground cover, along hedgerows, in vegetable gardens, and on undulating (or uneven) terrain. It is used widely under mulch or landscape bark to maximize water conservation as well as aesthetics. Pressure-compensating dripline allows use on slopes, hills, or rolling fields—application rates will remain consistent with watering requirements, and water will not be lost due to runoff or wind drift, which is common in overhead systems.

The dripline has a maximum length based on psi, emitter spacing, and flow rate. Opposite is a table showing maximum run lengths at various pressure for 0.5 and 1 gph dripline.

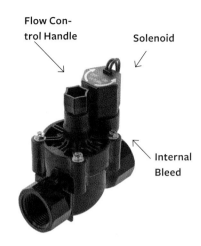

Flow Control Handle

Solenoid

Internal Bleed

Point Source or Inline Irrigation?

Deciding between point source emitters and dripline in your irrigation system depends on several factors, including the type of plants you're watering, the layout of your garden or landscape, and specific watering needs. Each method has its own set of advantages that make it suitable for different situations:

Use Point Source Emitters When:

- *Watering Individual Plants* Point source emitters are ideal for delivering water directly to the base of individual plants, trees, or shrubs—especially those with specific water requirements. This method ensures that each plant receives a precise amount of water, minimizing waste.

- *Variable Plant Spacing* In gardens where plants are spaced irregularly or far apart, point source emitters allow you to customize the watering to each plant without overwatering the areas in between.

- *Container Gardening* Point source emitters provide targeted watering directly to the container for potted plants or container gardens, ensuring adequate moisture without the need for a broader system that could lead to overwatering.

- *Landscapes with Mixed Plant Types* If your landscape includes a mix of plant types with varying water needs, point source emitters can be adjusted to deliver different flow rates, catering to each plant's unique requirements.

- *Sloped or Uneven Terrain* On sloped or uneven terrain, point source emitters can be more easily controlled to prevent runoff, allowing water to soak into the soil where it's needed.

Use Dripline When:
- *Watering Dense Plantings* Dripline is best suited for areas with closely spaced plants, such as vegetable gardens, flower beds, or dense ground covers. The continuous line of emitters ensures even watering across the entire area.

- *Creating an Efficient Watering System for Rows of Plants* For row crops or long beds of plants, dripline can provide uniform water distribution, ensuring each plant along the line receives an equal amount of water.

- *Reducing Weed Growth* Dripline irrigation can help reduce weed growth by concentrating water directly where it's needed for the plants, rather than watering the entire soil surface.

- *Minimizing Evaporation* Dripline systems, especially when covered with mulch, can significantly reduce water loss due to evaporation by delivering water directly to the soil surface or just below it.

- *Establishing Low-Maintenance Lawns* For certain types of low-growing, dense ground covers or turf replacements, dripline buried beneath the surface can provide consistent, low-maintenance watering.

In designing a spray system for 200 square feet of turf with spray heads, there are only one or two correct ways to do it. By contrast, there are many ways to design and install a drip system properly, allowing for creativity while conserving water. It also allows you to use various parts left over from other projects.

Unlike the rigid structure often required by spray systems, especially in small turf areas where precision is critical, and options are limited, drip irrigation offers a canvas for innovation. This flexibility not only encourages the conservation of our most precious resource, water but also allows for the utilization of various components you might have on hand from previous projects. By designing and installing a drip irrigation system in your garden, you're not just nurturing your plants; you're participating in a sustainable gardening practice that is as good for the planet as it is for your green space. So, gather those spare parts, let your creativity flow, and embark on the rewarding journey of creating a drip irrigation system that is uniquely yours. It's an opportunity to make a positive impact on your environment while enjoying the process of crafting a garden that thrives.

Acknowledgments

To my wife, Devonna Hall.

Your unwavering support and belief in my writing have always inspired me. You've encouraged my creative pursuits and nurtured my love for gardening. The countless hours we've spent together in the garden are among my most cherished moments, and I treasure every minute of that time with you. Thank you for filling my life with love, patience, and the beauty of nature.

This book reflects so many incredible people's support, knowledge, and encouragement. I want to thank those who significantly influenced my journey through the corporate world, irrigation industry, and digital media.

Bill Zingg, you were the first to teach me about irrigation. Your expertise was invaluable as I started, and I'll always appreciate your willingness to share your knowledge. Dave Palumbo, thank you for showing me how to multitask like a pro. Learning about valves while catching a Yankees World Series game will always be a fond memory. I still carry those irrigation lessons with me. Travis Bridges, our conversations deepened my knowledge of irrigation, and I gained a lasting friendship along the way. I'm grateful for both. Aric Olson, your faith in my creative ideas transformed many into water-saving solutions that made a real difference. Thank you for your trust and belief in my vision. Stuart Eyring, you've shown me what true enthusiasm for water conservation looks like, helping me see the bigger picture and inspiring me to keep pushing forward.

I am deeply thankful to the Master Gardener Association, especially Leah Taylor, its program coordinator, for helping spread the message of water conservation and providing hands-on training to thousands of passionate gardeners.

To my customers, thank you for listening, trusting, and believing that we can achieve meaningful water conservation together.

Roger Zino, you quickly saw the potential in a water management division and taught me the importance of getting the job done. Your foresight and drive have left a lasting impression on me. Dave Hanson, your energy and unwavering confidence in me over the years were priceless. Our Friday-afternoon discussions and your guidance were instrumental in turning ideas into action. Eric Santos, thank you for keeping the water-saving promises I made to customers. Your dedication made those promises a reality.

Stacee Gravelle Lawrence, I couldn't have navigated this book process without you. Thank you for your patience and attention to every detail. And to Kelley Galbreath and the full team at Rizzoli, many thanks for helping my book take such an attractive physical form and for helping it reach a wide readership.

I especially thank John Balzarini, who helped me master customer communication and achieve professional goals with confidence and clarity. Ken Mills, you opened my eyes to the strategic side of the irrigation business, and I am forever grateful for that. Charles Fishman, your ability to make water a fascinating topic continues to inspire me, and I am thankful for your insights.

To the irrigation sales teams I've worked with, you showed me the true power of teamwork in driving water conservation forward. It was a privilege to be part of these teams.

To the many guests on my webinars, you taught me—and our audience—so much about water conservation and sustainability. Your expertise helped shape this journey.

Jim Lauria and John Petroso, your ideas were informative and entertaining, making conversations about water engaging and fun.

Andrew Brennan, thank you for greenlighting my first blog. That step opened countless doors and opportunities for growth.

And to Lauren Proctor, you taught me everything I know about digital media and how to craft an exciting message. Your guidance has been invaluable throughout this process.

To all of you—thank you for helping me bring this book to life and for your unwavering support in spreading the message of water conservation.

Photo Credits

Appendix

Plant Hardiness Zones by Country

USDA ZONE	RHS ZONE (UK)	AUS ZONE	TEMPERATURE RANGES °F (°C)	CATEGORY
13	H1a	7	Warmer than 59 (15)	Heated glasshouse/greenhouse—tropical
12	H1b	6	50 to 59 (10 to 15)	Heated glasshouse/greenhouse—subtropical
11	H1c	5	41 to 50 (5 to 10)	Heated glasshouse/greenhouse—warm temperate
10b	H2	4	34 to 41(1 to 5)	Tender—cool or frost-free glasshouse/greenhouse
9b/10a	H3	3	23 to 34 (-5 to 1)	Half-hardy—unheated glasshouse/greenhouse / mild winter
8b/9a	H4	2	14 to 23 (-10 to -5)	Hardy—average winter
7b/8a	H5	1	5 to 14 (-15 to -10)	Hardy—cold winter
6b/7a	H6		-4 to 5 (-20 to -15)	Hardy—very cold winter
6a–1	H7		Colder than -4 (<-20)	Very hardy

Useful Websites

Land-Grant Colleges and Universities: Many of these have agricultural or co-operative extensions that can provide information tailored to local conditions to home gardeners. https://www.nifa.usda.gov/about-nifa/how-we-work/partnerships/land-grant-colleges-universities

USDA PLANTS Database: https://plants.usda.gov

Irrigation Association Water Budgeting Tools and Calculators: https://www.irrigation.org/IA/Resources/Tools-Calculators/Water-Budgeting

Environmental Protection Agency (EPA) Water Budget Data Finder: https://www.epa.gov/watersense/water-budget-data-finder

National Weather Service (NWS) Experimental Forecast Reference EvapoTranspiration (FRET) Information: https://www.weather.gov/cae/fretinfo.html

For the author's product recommendations and more, visit: http://h2otrends.com/shop/

The Penman-Monteith Equation

The Penman-Monteith equation is the most common method for calculating ETo and is based on meteorological measurements. These include temperature, humidity, wind speed, solar radiation, and cloud cover. Measuring these multiple factors at once gives this method high accuracy. The Food and Agriculture Organization of the United Nations recognizes it as the standard method to use for water management.

The Penman-Monteith equation is a complex mathematical formula that calculates ETo based on various meteorological parameters. The equation is expressed as follows below.

The Penman-Monteith equation is used to estimate the rate of water loss due to evapotranspiration. By knowing the ETo value for a specific location and time, farmers and irrigation specialists can determine the water requirements of their crops. This information guides irrigation scheduling to ensure crops receive adequate moisture without overwatering. ETo values are typically used as a reference point for creating irrigation schedules. Gardeners can adjust irrigation frequency based on ETo data, weather forecasts, and plant factors to optimize water use and plant health. This helps prevent both under- and over-irrigation.

$$ET_o = \frac{\Delta(R_n-G)}{\lambda[\Delta + \gamma(1+C_dU_2)]} + \frac{\gamma\dfrac{37}{T_a + 273.16} U_2(e_s+e_a)}{\Delta + \gamma(1+C_dU_2)} \qquad \text{(EQ1)}$$

Where:

ET_o = grass reference evapotranspiration (mm h^{-1})

Δ = slope of saturation vapor pressure curve (kPa °C^{-1})at mean air temperature (T)

R_n = net radiation (MJ m^{-2} h^{-1})

G = soil heat flux density (MJ m^{-2} h^{-1})

γ = physchometric constant (kPa °C^{-1})

T_a = mean hourly air temperature (°C)

U_2 = wind speed at 2 meters (m s^{-1})

e_s = saturation vapor pressure (kPa) at the mean hourly air temperature (T) in °C

e_a = actual vapor pressure (kPa) at the mean hourly air temperature (T) in °C

lamda (λ) = latent heat of vaporization (MJ kg^{-1})

C_d = bulk surface resistance and aerodynamic resistance coefficient

Index